THE LETTERS OF
ALGERNON CHARLES SWINBURNE

POSTHUMOUS POEMS
of
ALGERNON CHARLES SWINBURNE
Edited by EDMUND GOSSE, C.B. and THOMAS JAMES WISE

Cloth, 8vo. $1.50 net

"Pretty well every mode of Swinburne's muse, every string of his lyre, is represented in this volume —the swaying sonorous metres, the gorgeous vesture, the familiar reiterated imagery, the familiar themes."
—*New York Times Book Review.*

John Lane Company   New York

The Letters of Algernon Charles Swinburne

Edited by
Edmund Gosse, C.B.
and
Thomas James Wise

Vol. II

NEW YORK: JOHN LANE COMPANY
LONDON: WILLIAM HEINEMANN
MCMXIX

COPYRIGHT, 1919.
BY JOHN LANE COMPANY

Press of
J. J. Little & Ives Company
New York, U.S.A.

LETTER I

To Lord Houghton

*Holmwood,
Henley-on-Thames.
March 13th, 1877.*

MY DEAR LORD HOUGHTON,
On returning last evening from the Isle of Wight, where my father was buried on Saturday beside a daughter whom he lost at Bonchurch in 1863, I found among others your kind word of sympathy awaiting me, for which I was sincerely and cordially grateful. Among friends for whose acquaintance I am in debt to your own good offices, I have also had very kind letters from Mrs. Greville and from dear old Mrs. Proctor; and among others from my father's co-eval friend and old schoolmaster, Sir Walter Trevelyan. I had always hoped and expected—Mr. Jowett said the same thing in his reply to a note in which I sent word of our loss to him, who had been our guest here just two months before—that my father would have remained with us longer in continued enjoyment of life (for enjoyment he had of it really to the last); but he never quite got over the blow he sustained

last summer by the death of his cousin and closest lifelong friend, Sir Henry Gordon, whose marriage with a sister of my mother made the bond between them still more like that between an elder and a younger brother, and whose painfully sudden death, reversing their anticipated parts, and laying on my father the cares of an executor to the will of his junior, involved him in more "labour" as well as "sorrow" than the strongest man who has "come to fourscore years" can well be expected to support.

Ever sincerely yours,
A. C. SWINBURNE.

A trivial little note of mine on a small personal matter appeared in last week's *Athenæum*.[1]

LETTER II

To NORMAN MACCOLL

Holmwood,
Henley-on-Thames.
March 30th, 1877.

MY DEAR MR. MACCOLL,
I begin this letter without knowing how I shall direct it—whether or not to "Freshwater"

---

[1] A letter to the Editor of *The Athenæum* refuting the statement that any of the pieces in *Poems and Ballads*, 1866, had been suppressed.

tout court, as in the address of your last letter. But in any case I hope you will get it, if not before, then on your return to London.

I am afraid I must have muddled what I had to say about the type and position of my Essay [1] —which was, and is, simply that I thought, and think, it should appear—by no means among the reviews—but in a type distinct from that of the correspondence and notes to which you will not be surprised to receive this week a contribution [2] of some length and outspokenness from me in reply to Mr. Furnivall's characteristic—and therefore grossly insolent—reference to me in his letter of to-day on Chaucer. The bargee in *Codlingsby* "liked w'opping a lord," and I rather like doing the same kind office for a pedant.

I hope I may get a proof of this reply without delay; for accuracy is specially important in such a case, and until I have answered, and publicly chastised, such a sample of unprovoked impertinence, all the French and Irish particles of my blood tingle with an instinct answering to that of Bussy d'Amboise or Sir Lucius O'Trigger.

I think—if you will allow me to say, or care to know that I think so—you were perfectly right

[1] A study of Victor Hugo's *La Sieste de Jeanne,* which appeared in *The Athenæum* for Feb. 24, 1877, p. 257.
[2] A letter headed *The Court of Love,* printed in *The Athenæum* for April 14, 1877. Reprinted in *Letters to the Press,* 1912, pp. 44-50.

and wise to avoid any notice of my *Swallow*,[1] which might have exposed *The Athenæum* to the charge of personal or private puffery—an imputation to which the silence of all other papers on the subject might undoubtedly, as you say, have laid it open; the net result of which must have been harm all round, and no good to anyone.

To return to the "typical" question for one last moment. I am not quite clear in my mind what the word "leading" means. Does it or not mean printing in larger type—or what?[2] "Aperiently so," as Mrs. Gamp has it; and if so, that is all I ever dreamed of asking.

Now I drop the pen to resume the lash. You shall have a letter worthy of Junius; Dunce Furnivall, a flagellation worthy of Orbilius; which, if you have read his impudence, you will allow is as much beneath his deserts as the discipline of Dr. Busby would have been beneath the deserts of Dr. Oates.[3]

Yours faithfully,
A. C. SWINBURNE.

[1] *The Sailing of the Swallow,* printed in *The Gentleman's Magazine,* March 1877, pp. 287-308. Reprinted in *Tristram of Lyonesse and other Poems,* 1882, pp. 13-40, where the piece forms the first Canto of the title-poem.

[2] "Leading"—to insert thicker slips of type-metal between the lines of type, thus rendering the printed text more legible, and giving it a bolder effect.

[3] The quarrel (mainly upon minor Shakespeare matters) carried on for so long a period in the public press by Swinburne

LETTER III

To Edmund Gosse

Holmwood.
April 1st, 1877.

My dear Gosse,

In spite of this ominous date—one which is (to say the least) of irreverent significance and profane suggestiveness for the anniversary of the highest Christian festival—you need fear no deception in the assurance that I shall be much gratified by your citation of my "Ballade" (the only one I believe extant in English). I am glad you saw and liked my latest printed version from Villon—but worse (and better) in the same line remains behind: notably a version of the famous and incomparable gallows-ballad, and one of the appeal to his friends and fellow-rascals—poets, pimps, and pick-purses—from the condemned cell. When I come to town you must come and hear me read them.

Kindest regards to you both from
Yours ever sincerely,
A. C. Swinburne.

and Furnivall, in the course of which the latter styled the former (in print) *Pigsbrook,* whilst the former styled the latter (but never in print) *Brothelsdyke,* is one of the least happy portions of Swinburne's at all times interesting and vivid correspondence.

LETTER IV

To Edmund Gosse

Holmwood.
April 4th, [1877].

MY DEAR GOSSE,
I write (not only to acknowledge your note, but) to ask—as you are writing on the naturalization of foreign metres in English—if you know my sestina printed on the first page of the 1872 (I *think*—*2,* not 1 or 3) volume of *Once a Week*,[1] to which F. Locker got me to send it (like a fool), and *from* which I never to this day (the day preceding my ——th—say fifty-fifth birthday) have received one penny in discharge of my humble earnings as "a honest tradesman." (Perhaps you will infer—wrongly—that a rankling reminiscence of this transaction has injuriously affected my estimate of socio-comic or comico-social poets in general—Dobson included—of whom I hardly know enough to like or dislike his work, but am quite prepared to hope you may be right in your approval of it—tho' I cannot imagine the best of it equal to Praed's best things for *distinction*—the one necessary crowning quality of such work.)

[1] *Sestina* ("*I saw my soul at rest upon a day*") printed in *Once a Week,* January 6, 1872.

But that poor, lost, still-born and buried sestina of mine (which is, of course, as much at your service as the ballade if required) is one of my very best short things—*much* better than Rizzio's in *Bothwell*. And nobody shall tell me I didn't invent the rhyming sestina—a new variation which delighted Rossetti—both in English and French—(and nobody yet has ever tried it, I believe, in Italian), a fact worth noting in your paper if you cite me as an innovator. I really am ashamed to say I don't know—or have forgotten—but what *is* a "chant royal"?

Look into the *Athenæum* this week if you want to witness one of the soundest flagellations ever conferred on a howling churl—this time administered by the hand of

                Yours very sincerely,
                    A. C. SWINBURNE.

Really this scrawl is worthy of poor dear old Landor, for splotchy shakiness!

LETTER V

TO EDMUND GOSSE

Holmwood.
April 6th, 1877.

MY DEAR GOSSE,
    Many thanks to you both for your birthday wishes and gift, which I shall value very much and regard as an additional inducement drawing me to London at the end of this month or opening of next.

I did *not* see your mention of my *sixtines, apropos* of the Comte de Grammont[1]—"who in the name of Hamilton is he?" and when did it appear? I (now) want very much to see it.

I am in as damnable a temper this morning as ever I was in my life (which is saying a good deal), or as ever Mr. Landor was in his (which is saying a good deal more) on the receipt of a note from MacColl postponing the appearance of my flagellant note (on Dunce Furnivall, *of course*) till next week, and suggesting even its suppression, as superfluous. To this I have replied that if it does not appear next week without fail I shall

[1] The Comte de Grammont introduced the *sestina* or *sextine* into modern French poetry, and between 1830 and 1848 wrote a large number of examples, which he included in his volume *Le Chant du Passé* (1854).

accept the unmistakable hint that he wishes never to see a line from my hand in the columns of his paper again. I am DAMNED if I put up with this sort of thing at any time. I got the proof yesterday morning all right without a word accompanying it—corrected it and despatched the condemned thing by a blighted express messenger to the nearest sanguinary post town—four Bulgarian miles—in time to catch the first Tartarian train to the God-doomed metropolis of this hell-devoted country—and this (as Mr. Carlyle would say) is the Gomorrah-like result.[1]

The composition of that last Ciceronian (if not Demosthenic) sentence has given me some slight and inadequate relief—but I am seriously *very* much irritated and vexed—not having boiled milk in my veins (unluckily for me), but some infusion of Hotspur's lineal blood in direct descent; so you can hardly expect me to be *very* much weaker than a tame rabbit—*n'est ce pas?* And even milk would boil of itself twice over "at these indignities." *Passons.*

My sunflower poem, about which you ask (*Complaint of Monna Lisa*), was published (as I find on hunting it up) in the *Fortnightly Review* of Feb. 1870, Vol. VII (N.S.), pp. 176-180. Certainly, if you talk of metrical inventions or inno-

---

[1] *The Court of Love* duly appeared in *The Athenæum*, April 14, 1877.

vations, there is one of the hardiest on record—a reduplicated inter-rhyming sestina (dodicina, as Rossetti preferred to call it), the twelve rhymes carried on even into the *six*-line *envoy,* as you will find if you look close for them in the 4th and 10th syllables of each line of it—or simply if you (having a poet's ear) read it out. But it is not meet to throw pearls before Furnivalls, nor take the (Delian) children's bread and cast it to the British public. Mind you get the sestina sacrificed on the Grub Street altar of *Once a Week.* You are thoroughly right about the waste of tossing such things to the feeders on such rotten acorns and mouldy rye as *Epics of Hades* and the like. Who the Deity is the author—Louis or *Lyewis* Morris? Tennyson's under-butler?

That ballade you like so much is about the only lyric I couldn't do straight off the minute I wanted —the verses *jibbed* like horses new to harness, and wouldn't come up to the rhymes all right—so after half-an-hour's pulling at them I went to bed in a rage, later by that half-hour than usual—dismissed all thought of verses, and woke next morning all right, and went and wrote the thing off when I got up exactly as it now stands.

Did you ever see the (now unprocurable) works of two early mediæval French poets (one privately printed—the other in a limited edition)—the Vidame de Chartres (I paraphrased a spring song of his long ago [1]), and Jehannot de Lescurel, who had a good deal of Keats in him, a lyrist of about Chaucer's date (I think), or Lydgate's at latest, if not earlier? The latter is exquisite—as perfect a *bird* among human singers as ever flew. The Vidame wouldn't go to the Crusades because he could not bear to leave the land where his lady was, and she cut him dead because he was the only knight who shirked.

Ever yours,
A. C. SWINBURNE.

[1] The reference is to the beautiful lyric beginning "When the fields catch flower," in the *Poems and Ballads* of 1866, and there said to be "from the French of the Vidame de Chartres, 12—?" Some of Swinburne's earliest readers believed this to be one of his mystifications, and it has not been found possible to identify the poet. In mediæval times, however, Chartres possessed a *vidamé,* though what was the name of the particular Vidame seems difficult to discover. No such obscurity attends Jehannot de Lescurel, a French poet of the 14th century, whose *Chansons, Ballades et Rondeaux,* were published in 1855, from a MS. source, by A. de Montaiglon, in a little 16mo, which is now of excessive rarity.

LETTER VI

To Norman MacColl

*3, Great James St.,
W.C.
[Friday, June,* 1877].

DEAR MR. MACCOLL,
 I send you a sort of half-letter half-essay on the subject of a book much discussed of late. Why I should write a word on the subject the semi-personal reason given at starting will explain. I have just read it to Watts, who approves of it highly, having read one or two pages of M. Zola's charming book which I selected as samples for his delectation. I have made the language of my work inadequately soft, and on the whole I thought it would look too like a "puff oblique" (and God knows it is not meant for that) to make mention of the one redeeming passage I could remember.

Yours sincerely,
A. C. SWINBURNE.

**
*

 The above letter covered Swinburne's lengthy article denouncing the tone of Zola's *L'Assommoir,* first printed in *The Athenæum,* and reprinted in *Letters to the Press,* 1912, pp. 51-57.

LETTER VII

To Edmund Gosse

> 3, *Great James Street,*
> *W.C.*
> *June 5th,* [1877].

My dear Gosse,
  Many thanks for your present of Dobson's poems.[1] I agree with you that some of them are charming bits of workmanship. Others (*e.g. Autonoë*—which is praised in the *Examiner,* and seems to me very poor stuff) I do not care for. The villanelle to "Rose" is exquisite.

I want you to come some day soon and hear me read an essay on Charlotte Brontë, which was my chief occupation or diversion last winter, when I was not up to much in the way of verse. Will Saturday evening between 7 and 8 suit you?
  Ever yours,
  A. C. Swinburne.

[1] *Proverbs in Porcelain:* by Austin Dobson [1877].

LETTER VIII

To Edmund Gosse

3, *Great James Street,*
W.C.
June 13*th,* [1877].

My dear Gosse,
    I take a big sheet of paper to lay a big project before you, which has long been "hovering in my restless head," as our young father Marlowe has it. Could not you and one or two more combine with me to write a *Dictionary of the English Drama*—critical and historical, biographical and bibliographic at once? The existing Biographia Dramatica was even in its own day a byword for scandalous incompetence—and to *this* day there is no other book of reference on the subject in the language. At least there should be such an one extending from Marlowe to Shirley. After the B. Restoration, I could take to my own hand no more than Dryden, Congreve (but with him I have briefly dealt twice already), Vanbrugh—and perhaps Farquhar and Sheridan. In the P. R. or Pre-Restoration period I have already said my say in full on Beaumont and Fletcher, Ford and Chapman—as you yours on Webster: and could only (even were this feasible) repeat or condense what had already appeared. The book—at what-

ever date we are to fix its limit—ought to be as nearly exhaustive as possible, but rigid in its observance of proportion—allowing to each name exactly as much space as it was intrinsically worth.

Send—or, better far, bring me word what you think of my scheme. I have not yet named it to any one—but no doubt Chatto would jump at it—at least I should hope so.

With best regards to Mrs. Gosse, and thanks for a really charming (tho' Sunday) afternoon.
Yours ever,
A. C. SWINBURNE.

LETTER IX

To Edmund Gosse

June 13th, [1877] (again).

MY DEAR GOSSE,
    Since I wrote this morning I have seen Chatto and he *jumped* at my idea of the *Biog. Dram.*, so if you will take a share in the enterprise and its profits (pecuniary or literary, possible or certain) please let me know at once.
Ever yours,
A. C. SWINBURNE.

LETTER X

To Edmund Gosse

> 3, *Great James Street,*
> *W.C.*
> *Monday, September* 18th, [1877].

MY DEAR GOSSE,
　　I can just manage painfully to scrawl one line of hearty congratulation [1] to you both, and to express a wish that I may before very long make the young lady's acquaintance, and congratulate *her* on her choice of hair-dye, which I take as a personal compliment on her part—as you say it is "my colour"!
　　Yours enviously but affectionately,
　　　　　　　　　A. C. SWINBURNE.

LETTER XI

To Edmund Gosse

> 3, *Great James Street,*
> *W.C.*
> *September* 21st, [1877].

MY DEAR GOSSE,
　　Tho' I am afraid it must be too soon to ask *when* I may be allowed to call—deeply as I

---
[1] On the birth of an eldest daughter.

always desire to pay early homage to any fresh Incarnation of the God Baby—I must write a line to express the pleasure with which I have this minute read your brief but terse and "pregnant" article on Unsaint Cyril [1] (as I call him, borrowing old Carlyle's delightful phrase of "Unsaint Ignatius"—meaning Loyola), as *versus* the old martyred saint of that name—an admirable corrective of the dolorously inadequate and incompetent notice in last week's *Anthenæum*.

But I must say I agree with Collins—or rather I believe it is he who agrees with me—that *The Atheist's Tragedy* is palpably and indisputably earlier than *The Revenger's*—which, so far from being neglected, like Wells's *Joseph,* ran through three editions in three years—1607-8-9—a success which I should be well content if any of my poor works would emulate, and which, I need not remind you, is as rare among printed plays of the time as a white thrush or a pink diamond. I have no doubt but that the almost unexampled success of Vindici induced some enterprising publisher to resuscitate the dead (and presumably damned) D'Amville. As to the style of the plays, I think you ought to have observed that so far from imitating Marston in that point Tourneur writes in both tragedies with the most exquisite simplicity, clarity and purity; while Marston, alone among

[1] Cyril Tourneur, the Elizabethan dramatist.

our dramatists, writes—at least during his first or "Crispinus" period—almost in the style (now and then) of the *Transformed Metamorphosis*—a poem which on a first reading seemed well-nigh to have affected me with incipient softening of the brain.

"Kiss the" Babe—not "Son" but Daughter in this case—"lest it be angry," in my name for once—I wonder when I shall be permitted to salute her "little godship" (as Coleridge says)?—and with all cordial regards to the Mother and yourself,

Believe me,
Ever yours,
A. C. SWINBURNE.

LETTER XII

To JOHN CHURTON COLLINS

Middle Cliff,
Southwold,
Wangford.
September 22nd, [1877?].

MY DEAR COLLINS,

I found your (undated) letter at my rooms on the 20th, the day on which you were to return to London, and on the evening of which I was in hopes of seeing you, but could not manage, having but a very few and busy hours in town. Had I been sure of an address that would find you, I should have sent you before now the papers which Watts has in charge for you—my own, and (more important) Mr. Grosart's "notes and queries" on the proof text of Tourneur's luminous and graceful poem.[1]

I really think the interpretation suggested in his commentary (which in place of transcribing I send you as it stands in the original shape of two private letters to me, of which you will see that you are at liberty and welcome to make any use you please as editor) a masterpiece of almost miraculous ingenuity, considering the portentous and ineffable nature of the undertaking; and having found such an Oedipus I hope the Cyrilian sphinx will cease to haunt your hag-ridden vigils or visions as a nightmare. The reverent commentator's own style is not exactly a model of pure classic English, and I suspect him of a certain kind of fellow-feeling for Cyril's ineffably and incredibly amorphous barbarisms. That his solution is generally right I have no doubt; but I decline to accept his correction and exposition of "the blessed word" "sinderesize." [2]

I hope your labours will soon be at an end, and

---

[1] The impenetrably obscure *Transformed Metamorphosis*.

[2] Collins observed that this hideous word is formed from συντήρησις, and defined it as "the pure part of conscience."

the edition out this year; also that I may find you in town when I repass in three or four weeks' time. I have not been idle this summer, and tho' the Shakespeare work has been so irregularly postponed and interrupted by various causes, I have another instalment of it ready in MS.

Ever yours sincerely,
A. C. SWINBURNE.

LETTER XIII

To Edmund Gosse

3, Great James Street,
W.C.
September 29th, [1877].

MY DEAR GOSSE,

Thanks for your note—none the less that I had already seen Yates in his character of beadle laying the lash on Buchanan's mangy hide. Let us hope that a cudgel or a "cat" such as that wielded by the editor of the *World* may haply make more impression on that currish cuticle than the rapier or the horsewhip of higher and finer satire.

Ever yours,
A. C. SWINBURNE.

LETTER XIV

To Charles Augustus Howell

*3, Great James Street,
W.C.
October 8th,* [1877].

My dear Howell,

I should have answered your friendly note some time ago had I not been prostrate for weeks beneath the double scourge of sore throat and indigestion, which have kept me days together in bed at the mercy of a God "whom 'twere gross flattery to call a Marquis." I should be delighted to make the acquaintance of the young lady you mention; but as for the godfatherhood, you must remember that sponsorship is hardly in my line—unless indeed I might choose the "promises and vows" to be made on the child's behalf, and in fact conduct the service myself extempore—which might hardly meet the views of the parents. None the less am I flattered and honoured by the invitation,

And remain,
Yours sincerely,
A. C. SWINBURNE.

LETTER XV

To Edmund Gosse

October 9th, [1877].

My dear Gosse,

I have got a perfectly tremendous idea about the new Biog. Dram. Why confine it to England? I should like of all things to undertake the French dramatists (most of them); I dare say William Rossetti would undertake the Italians, and Hueffer (perhaps) the Germans; you (if, as Watts urgently advises, we bring it down to our own time) your favourite Scandinavians; for the Spanish we could surely find someone competent; and if there are any Muscovites (dash and blank them), as I believe there are, we might apply to the Russophil Ralston. I must confess that one slight social comedy or farce translated by Mérimée from the Russian (which is all I know of their drama) seemed to me when I read it very witty, original, and amusing.

Send me a line in answer, if only to say on what day at what hour I may "for sure" (as we say northwards) be admitted to do my bit of Divine Service at the altar of Baby.

Ever yours,
A. C. Swinburne.

Vide P.S. inside.

P.S.—I have just been trying on Watts's recommendation to read Mrs. Centlivre; but I must say for the most part she seems to me as dull as dishwater and as monotonous as a bagpipe.

I have lately had two noble windfalls in the way of dramatic bibliophily (if there is such a word): Rowley's *All's Lost by Lust,* of which hitherto I knew only the noble excerpts given by Lamb; and *Nobody and Somebody* (1600) with Charles I.'s autograph.

LETTER XVI

To Edmund Gosse

October 15*th,* [1877].

My dear Gosse,

Your friend Mr. Dobson is welcome to make any excerpts he pleases from any of my volumes; but I must consult Chatto as to the advisability of allowing the reproduction in such a form of a poem which has never yet been included in any collection of my lyrics, and is to reappear in the next forthcoming. Thus the *Ballad of Dreamland* stands on a different footing from the others proposed for selection, and the question is one for the publisher rather than the author to decide.

SWINBURNE'S LETTERS

If you will name a day and hour (bar next Wednesday evening) I will come to see your Dutch engravings with pleasure, but far more in hopes to be at length admitted to do personal homage at the shrine of Baby—

"a god
Worth many books and pictures."

Ever yours,
A. C. SWINBURNE.

LETTER XVII

To Edmund Gosse

[*January 8th, 1878.*]

MY DEAR GOSSE,
 I have mislaid your note of invitation and hunted (and set poor old Mrs. Magill hunting) for it, hours together. But my impression is that I was asked to dine with the Baby and the Cat (to say nothing of Mrs. Gosse and yourself) on Sunday at one, *punctually* (as if I was ever unpunctual!), which I shall be delighted to do. The Grosvenor Gallery[1] has fairly swept away

---

[1] The Grosvenor Gallery, which had been first opened to the public on May 1, 1877, had a winter exhibition, that same year, of drawings by the Old Masters. Over these Swinburne was in ecstasies. The show was one, at that time, unparalleled in the annals of English art. Swinburne was entranced by

such small remains of sanity as I possessed before going there—first with the Madox Browns, and secondly by myself. One cannot stand such a dose of Paradise all at once.

>Ever yours affectionately,
>A. C. SWINBURNE.

By the by, have you seen my Blake's *Hayley's Ballads,* bought last autumn? They are beyond all words. It is an awful pity there was not a copy at the Burlington last year.

LETTER XVIII

To Lord Houghton

>3, *Great James Street.*
>*February 22nd,* [1878].

MY DEAR LORD HOUGHTON,
    Arrived in town this morning after spending a month at Glasgow with Nichol. During this month I have completed for the press the last instalment of my forthcoming volume —*Poems and Ballads, Second Series,* with a dedicatory poem addressed—in fulfilment of a nine year old pledge—to our friend Burton; I have

the Raffaelles and the Peruginos, and most of all by some silverpoints of women's heads, by Leonardo da Vinci, to which he announced his intention of dedicating a cycle of sonnets.

secured a most superb copy of the now *introuvable et impayable* edition of the *Contes* of La Fontaine, illustrated by Eisen (l'édition des fermiers-généraux), of which the original plates were (as of course you know) recently destroyed by that man (or dog) of God, M. Veuillot.

I have published four sonnets on the war in the Glasgow newspaper,[1] of which five hundred copies were sold before noon on the morning of publication; I have consequently been preached at or verbally swished by a pedagogue parson (the Rev. F[lunkey] W[horeson] Farrar) . . . in public before a numerous congregation of both sexes in the principal church of Glasgow; for which I trust that Mr. Gladstone (unless first sent by a genuinely reformed government to the guillotine—whither may God speed him! may I be there to see him "sneeze in the bag" à la Marat) will on his next return to power confer a bishopric . . .

Ever yours sincerely,
A. C. SWINBURNE.

[1] *The White Czar* and *Rispah,* printed in *The Glasgow University Magazine,* No. 2, February, 1878.

LETTER XIX

To Edmund Gosse

April 5th, [1878].

My best love and thanks to the sweetest and kindest of babies for its birthday attention.[1] It is a sad fact that I have nothing as fragrant and beautiful to offer in return; but how should I, being a miserable adult, have any means of acknowledging the infinite sweetness and goodness and graciousness of a baby?

A. C. SWINBURNE.

LETTER XX

To John H. Ingram

3, *Great James St.,*
W.C.
April 10th, 1878.

MY DEAR SIR,

I am most sincerely obliged to you (not for the first time now, by many) for letting me know of a seeming neglect or discourtesy (were such a thing possible, as I trust it is not) on my

---

[1] A bunch of white roses sent to the poet on his birthday in the name of Teresa Gosse.

part towards a lady to whom I hold myself already under no small obligation for her exquisite rendering of my *Pilgrims*. Will you add yet again to your past kindness by assuring Mlle. Holmès that I never received a line from her hand on the subject mentioned—or any other? and that in either case I should have been as incapable as any other gentleman of leaving her letter unacknowledged—but that I entreat her to receive my fullest and most sincere apologies for the mere appearance of such a scandalous oversight as the omission to answer her letter? And will you further assure her that, as nothing could have pained or vexed me more than the very seeming or suspicion of such insolence and ingratitude, so I could scarcely receive a higher honour or a truer pleasure than I should feel to be conveyed by any further translations which it might please her to publish of any among my poems?

Believe me meantime, while as yet anxiously and eagerly awaiting the appearance of the promised paper in *The Athenæum,* which is to convey the Master's judgment on the unworthy subject of myself,[1]

Yours gratefully and sincerely,
A. C. SWINBURNE.

---

[1] It had been Victor Hugo's intention to write some lines on Swinburne, and send them to *The Athenæum* for publication.

LETTER XXI

To John H. Ingram

[*Postmark, London, W.C.*]
May 27th, [1878].
7.45 *p.m.*

Dear Mr. Ingram,
    I have been a bedridden invalid for many days—this being the first I have crawled out into the open air—but I think this summons would raise me like a second Lazarus from the very grave.[1] If it be physically possible, I will go. But I hardly think I could manage the journey alone so soon. Are you going? and (excuse the freedom), if so, could we go together? I could not of course ask you for the *petits soins d'un frère nourricier*—it is simply that even in robust health solitary travelling with all its attendant worries and bewilderments (which are nothing when divided) always brings on with me something like a mild fit of hypochondria.

Is it asking too much of your kindness (as I can hardly decide without seeing you) to say how truly kind and friendly it would be if you could

---

[1] An invitation from Victor Hugo, forwarded through Mr. Ingram, asking Swinburne as the representative of English poetry, to be present at the Centenary Commemoration of the death of Voltaire.

manage to look in here again to-morrow between 1 and 2 and share my luncheon and talk it over?
Yours sincerely,
A. C. SWINBURNE.

P.S.—By the by, I see in your last letter that you mention an application of Mlle. Holmès to me, proposing to do me the greatest and most gratifying honour of translating some of my poems into French, which had never received any reply. I hope and trust—nay, I am certain—that you have already anticipated the truth—namely, that I not only never received her letter, but never heard of it till now from you. Pray let the lady—at all events—know and be assured of this.
A. C. S.

LETTER XXII

To Lord Houghton

Holmwood.
July 11th, [1879].

DEAR LORD HOUGHTON,
My mother has just shown me your note to her inquiring after my health; so I add a line of acknowledgment to her reply. I *was* very unwell for weeks together before I left Lon-

don, and a good deal reduced in strength by prolonged insomnia and consequent loss of appetite and exhaustion; but a day or two at a friend's house near Putney Heath, with plenty of walking exercise thereon and thereabouts, sufficed to set me up—higher I may say than I had been for many months. Thence I came down here to see the last of this place, which we leave for good in October.

I am steadily working at my book on Shakespeare, and am in the pangs of travail for a better title than the one prefixed to the two first instalments in the *Fortnightly* some four years ago. Also I have the skeleton of the four remaining acts of *Mary Stuart* (Part 3rd) completely drawn out and jointed together (the first act has been some time in type) and hope to begin getting the bare bones clothed with flesh and sinews before long. (As Gray said of his Greek studies—"I take prose and poetry together like bread and cheese.") The trial scene at Fotheringhay (Act 3rd) will be the *crux,* owing to its necessary length, and the excess of material supplied to my hand by the fullness of the report. I must stew it all down into one scene, and condense the work of three days into one. For the rest, I have hit on a dramatic *motif* which will score at once as a connecting link between this and the two parts

preceding, and as a good solid hinge for the dramatic movement of the third.
Yours very truly,
A. C. SWINBURNE.

P.S.—I was all the more gratified by the mention of Mr. Browning's name in your letter to my mother, that, having received no copy of his new book [*Dramatic Idyls* I.] which I have read with great admiration and enjoyment, I had begun to fear he might have taken some offence at my seeming neglect last year (if I remember the date rightly—it may have been the year before! but I think not) to acknowledge with due thanks the receipt of his version of the *Agamemnon*. I do not know that I did so neglect my duty, but I certainly never heard of his having received the copy I ordered my publishers to send *him* in my name of my last volume of poetry.

A propos de bottes—and as everybody seems doomed nowadays to be always talking or writing about some theatrical matter—I was really and unaffectedly glad to see recorded in the papers (I forget how many months ago) the failure of Charles Reade's monstrous and incredible attempt to introduce on the English stage a dramatized version of the most horrible and loathsome book that ever got into type [*L'Assommoir*] . . . In a word, de Sade at his foulest was to Zola at his purest "as moonlight until sunlight and as water unto wine" in the faculty of horrifying and nauseating the human stomach and the human soul.

A. C. S.

Will you remember me to Mrs. Greville when occasion offers, and say I hope she received the presentation copy I ordered Chatto to send her of my last poems on their appearance a year ago? [*Poems and Ballads, Second Series.*]

LETTER XXIII

To Lord Houghton

Holmwood,
Shiplake,
Henley-on-Thames.
August 7th, 1879.

DEAR LORD HOUGHTON,
    Is there—oh! is there any truth in the report that in consequence of an article in *The Times* yesterday which decrees that there are—and shall be—no living poets in England, Mr. Tennyson and Mr. Browning have "shaken hands in death" by shutting themselves up in a hermetically sealed room with a pan of ignited charcoal between them? and that Mr. Thomas Carlyle,

regardless alike of his years, of the weather, and of the law of the land prohibiting indecent exposure, has been seen dancing a Highland fling, in a state of total nudity and partial intoxication, down and up the whole length of Cheyne Walk, Chelsea, with a Scotch cutty-pipe in his mouth, and the Scotch Fiddle on his back, by way of expressing as in a Pyrrhic war-dance the triumph of an "inarticulate poet" over the downfall of the last articulate individual of that ilk? But, alas! to whom am I, with my last faltering breath, appealing for information, which doubtless I must not—I dare not hope to receive? for you too, being one of us, the condemned victim of *The Times* guillotine and of *The Times* editor, Fouquier-Tinville petit-fils, are probably even now no more.

I wish I could find and copy out and send you a French love-song which I wrote some time ago —the first on record, I should think, that ever was addressed to an elderly London attorney— to Mr. Collette, Secretary and Solicitor to the Society for the Suppression of Vice (talk of *my* alliteration after that!). I need not remind you that Colette (with one *l*—I do not presume to guess what may or may not be signified by the reduplication of that liquid consonant) was a favourite name for a shepherdess of French love-songs of the last century, whether sentimental or *grivoises.* "Ma Collette," as I call it, is, I flatter myself, a pretty and tender little effusion, even if somewhat warm—I hope not unpardonably warm—in one or two of the closing stanzas.

Your friend Mr. Stedman turned up here a little before I got your letter introducing him, and was entertained to the best of my poor ability. He seems a very pleasant sort of man. We were breaking up (not for the holidays) and leave this place for good in a month or two.

I am very sorry indeed to have such a bad account from you of Burton. I had not heard from or of them for ages.

Ever sincerely yours,
A. C. SWINBURNE.

[It was not until February 2nd, 1880, that he found occasion to copy out the "Collette" verses for Lord Houghton, as follows:—]

STANCES À COLLETE

I

Ange ou fillette,
O ma poulette,
O ma Collette,
Chaste ou follette,
   Reçois ma foi!
Vierge et guerrière,
Aventurière,
Ou bien rosière,
Mon âme entière
   *Est toute à **toi**.*

2

Fille estimable,
On dit qu'à table
Ou sur le sable,
(Inexprimable
　Ravissement!)
Malgré ta mine
De chatte fine,
Ma blanche hermine,
Tu lis JUSTINE
　Assidument.

3

Auprès de Lise
Sous la remise
À l'ombre assise,
Quand Dieu s'épuise
　En plain été,
Souvent, sans fable,
Ta bouche affable
Rend trop aimable
Ton adorable
　Société.[1]

4

Hélas! pucelle
À l'âme belle,
Cette étincelle
Où donc est-elle?
　Où donc est-tu?
Ta face blême
Porte elle-même
Ton anathème—
Malheur suprême
　De la vertu!

　　　　　　　　　　BERQUIN FILS.

[1] For the Suppression of Vice?

SWINBURNE'S LETTERS

LETTER XXIV[1]

TO EDMUND GOSSE

*The Pines.
Putney Hill,
S.W.
October 6th,* [1879].

MY DEAR GOSSE,
  Keats I will gladly undertake; the other three I must decline, having said my say fully on Coleridge and Blake (would W. B. Scott undertake the latter, do you think? he would surely do it well), and neither knowing enough—by any means—of Chatterton, nor—on the whole—taking

[1] This letter, and those which immediately succeed it, refer to the project of four volumes of selections from *The English Poets,* with critical introductions by various writers, and a general introduction by Matthew Arnold, which was at this time entrusted by Messrs. Macmillan to Mr. Humphry Ward, and was completed in 1883. The suggestions of this first letter, as will appear, were not carried out; Keats was ultimately entrusted to Matthew Arnold, S. T. Coleridge to Walter Pater, Blake to J. Comyns Carr, and Chatterton to Watts-Dunton. Landor, it appeared, had already been offered to, and accepted by, Lord Houghton; an arrangement which did not please Swinburne entirely, although he was asked for and gave some advice regarding the selection, and consented to translate for the introduction a Latin epigram of Landor's. Why Swinburne did not write, after all, on Keats, is no longer remembered, but his only contribution to the collection was a very eloquent essay on, and a selection from, the poems of William Collins.

interest enough in him except as a splendid *lusus naturæ,* to deal adequately—that is, cordially, for without cordiality (which here I do not feel) there can be no thoroughness in such work—with the subject of his peculiar genius.

You have the finest list of contributors I ever heard of. Does the programme—otherwise shamefully imperfect on one point—include the name of Landor? If it does—and if Browning (whose claim would of course be prior to any man's) does not undertake him—if, under these circumstances, the task is assigned to any mortal soul but me—as Malvolio says, "I'll be revenged on the whole pack of you": nor shall any one "entreat me to a peace." Years upon years ago I drew out a list of his poems most suitable for selection; but the defunct Forster snuffed out my project with the announcement that he designed himself to do this office for his old friend's work; and as he and Browning were (I was told) co-legatees of all Landor's copyrights—a bequest, I should fear, not exactly equivalent to the legacy of a large income [1]—nothing could be done without them, as the man who was going to be hanged said of himself with regard to the impending cere-

---

[1] In the autumn of 1859, and for the remaining five years of the old man's stormy life, Browning generously took charge of Landor's affairs, having found him in Siena, "homeless, with nothing but the clothes he stood in, and a few pauls in his pocket."

mony. On the other hand Browning, for his part, long afterwards expressed in kind and cordial terms his earnest wish that I would carry out my original project, and even offered me his invaluable furtherance in doing so, by free leave to inspect and so put to use his Landorian rarities, unknown even to the British Museum (as *I* know from inspection of the catalogue). Possibly, however, his mind may have changed to me-ward, if I may judge from the shameful fact that he has accepted the shameful office of president over the most blackguardly gang of blockheads in Europe.

My Shakespeare book is almost halfway through the press. Just in time to insert a note of acclamation saluting the good news, I hear from our invaluable friend Dr. Grosart that he has discovered the phœnix's nest—the roc's egg of Shakespearean literature—a perfect copy all allegations as to the non-existence of such an one notwithstanding—of

Willobie His Avisa.[1]

[1] It was not until the spring of 1880 that Dr. Alexander B. Grosart published the treasure-trove of which Swinburne speaks here with so much enthusiasm. *Willobie His Avisa* (1594) proved, after all, something of a disappointment. Henry Willoughby, the hero of the poem, had a friend whose initials were W. S., and these were, perhaps too readily, supposed to refer to Shakespeare, whose "Mr. W. H.," it was thought, might be Henry Willoughby. The author of *Avisa* was one Hadrian Dorrell, otherwise unidentified, but the chamberfellow of "Willobie." But all the evidence is very thin and dim, and the poem itself excessively poor.

Of course you know what is the priceless and unique importance of that book in reference to Shakespeare's sonnets; and a (further) reference to the long discussion on the matter in old volumes of *Notes and Queries* will show you (if I mistake not) how universal was the belief—first communicated to me by a great collector of rarities now dead, who had an imperfect copy in most beautiful condition otherwise—that no single perfect copy of the priceless book was in existence.

Once more—no one could well confer on me a greater obligation than would be conferred by the man who should procure me the opportunity of editing the select poems of Landor; I could never forget such a service, as I should consider the occasion given me of rendering that service to the famous memory of a great man who glorified me for ever by the name of a friend.

Watts will have shown you the notes I took the liberty of pencilling on the margin of your poems in proof. Let me here, with all my heart and soul, congratulate you above all on the magnificent sonnet of *Alcyone*,[1] and say once for all the mere simple truth—that, with Shakespeare's, Milton's, Wordsworth's, and Rossetti's very finest sonnets in my memory, I regard you as the writer

[1] *New Poems* (1879).

of one among the noblest in this or in any (even in Dante's) language.

With kindest remembrance to Mrs. Gosse.

Yours ever,
A. C. SWINBURNE.

P.S.—You need not put Watts's name on my address any more than mine on his, as we have both moved in together.—A.C.S.

LETTER XXV

To Edmund Gosse

The Pines,
Putney Hill,
S.W.
October 10th, [1879].

MY DEAR GOSSE,

It is with no flavour of sour grapes on my tongue that I can say I would rather read Arnold on Keats than write on Keats myself. I only hope—but of this I gravely doubt—that his selection, and above all his arrangement of the selected poems, will be such as I should agree was the best and (to use his own favourite epithet) the most adequate possible. The prefatory essay is sure to be most exquisite reading—*merum sal cum mero melle.*

On Landor I could of course write my fill anywhere at any time; but in this case above all it is the adequacy of the representative selections which is the first and last thing to be looked to; and on that score I will yield precedence in competency to no man whatever.

On Byron I have not another word to say in public; finding nothing to add or recant, and little if anything to modify, on reconsideration of my early essay.

But one poet remains whom I should dearly like to edit, and would do my very best to do him full and late and necessary justice; and this is Collins. On him, if it were desired, I could fall to work almost at once. Excluding Blake from the list of properly and exclusively eighteenth century poets—(and among them, if we include all who published before 1800, we must class not only Blake, but Coleridge and Wordsworth!)—I hold Collins as *facile principem* in the most quintessential quality of a poet proper; and I should like to show reason why, by giving a rapid comparative estimate of all possible competitors for his crown.

Our indefatigable and invaluable friend Grosart is actually about to reprint a perfect copy of the *Avisa*—first edition (1594). Glory be to the Unknowable! Pray, if you can, get and send me a copy of your article on the *Phœnix and Turtle*.[1] I very much wish to read it.

As to Browning's having disgraced himself for life by his acceptance of a presidency of a blackguard's gang of blockheads, it is but an additional and perhaps superfluous proof that he is not thoroughbred gentleman enough to have the due self-respect which should—and does not—always accompany genius. I would rather see a copy of your answer to the head blackguard's impertinent offer [2] than even your aforesaid article. My own reply to the same proposal from the same foul quarter long since was of course—in Thomson's phrase—"expressive silence."

Pray tell Mrs. Gosse, with my kindest remembrances, how much honoured I am by her association of my poor song with my nursing mother's.[3]

[1] Shakespeare's poem, somewhat mysteriously published in 1601 by Robert Chester, in *Love's Martyr*.

[2] This vivacious allusion is to the fact that Robert Browning had accepted the presidency of the New Shakespeare Society, formed by F. J. Furnivall. What "the head blackguard's impertinent offer" may have been seems to be lost in the abyss of time. The conflict was extremely exhilarating to both the protagonists. A survivor can only remark that Furnivall began it, and that at the date of this letter he was slinging around postcards to Swinburne's friends on which the poet was archly described as *Pigsbrook*.

[3] Mrs. Gosse had told him that the sound of the sea on the black rocks of the Cornish coast had reminded her of *The Triumph of Time;* and he responds with an allusion to—

> *I will go back to the great sweet Mother,*
> *Mother and lover of men, the Sea.*

I once thought of a symbolical quasi-autobiographical poem after the fashion of Shelley or of Hugo, concerning the generation, birth and rearing of a by-blow of Amphitrite's—not even in dreams and symbols would I dare claim fellowsonship to Thetis with Pelides—reared like Ion in the temple-service of Apollo. It would be a pretty subject, but when should I hear the last of my implied arrogance and self-conceit?[1]

As to your own glorious *Alcyone,* allow a venerable senior but one piece of advice. Be not, like Drayton, the man of one immortal sonnet; nor, like Wordsworth and Rossetti, the man of too many to be otherwise than mortal in the main. With which, praying Our Father which is in Delphi to have you always in His Most Holy Keeping, I remain

Your fellow-servant,
A. C. SWINBURNE.

[1] This project, nevertheless, he presently carried out, in *Thalassius* (1880).

LETTER XXVI

To Edmund Gosse

The Pines,
Putney Hill,
S.W.
October 15*th,* [1879].

MY DEAR GOSSE,
    I cannot but write you a word of cordial thanks for a letter *not* addressed to me (tho' I mean to keep a copy of it for my private delectation and encouragement, as a "heartener" (should I ever need one) against public or private obloquy), of which Watts has just shown me the transcript you have sent him. You may like to know that it has come to cheer me at a moment when such a taste of manly and friendly sympathy is most especially welcome, for other and graver reasons than one special blackguard's ribaldry. As long as I can feel that I may count, and have a right to count, on the steady friendship and fidelity of honourable gentlemen, I will not for very shame's sake so far forget or forego my own claim to a sense of self-respect as to fret my heart-strings by day or by night over such disgusting facts as that I hear of one person [1] who was once

[1] Charles Augustus Howell.

my friend, and is yet my debtor, habitually amusing mixed companies of total strangers by obscene false anecdotes about my private eccentricities of indecent indulgence as exhibited in real or imaginary *lupanaria;* and of another,[1] who is now a thing unmentionable alike by men and women, as equally abhorrent to either—nay, to the very beasts—raising money by the sale of my letters to him in past years, which must doubtless contain much foolish burlesque and now regrettable nonsense never meant for any stranger's eye who would not understand the mere childishness of the silly chaff indulged in long ago. But if I may respectfully venture on a parody of the Psalmist, it is all right with me, and shall be, as long as I can say, "Men are on my side: I will not care what beasts may do unto me."

Yours ever sincerely,
A. C. SWINBURNE.

[1] Simeon Solomon.

SWINBURNE'S LETTERS

LETTER XXVII

TO EDMUND GOSSE

*The Pines,
Putney Hill,
S.W.
October 17th,* [1879].

MY DEAR GOSSE,

Evidently I am to die your debtor, and insolvent—for no gratitude can repay the friend who has been the instrument of procuring for me the satisfaction of a desire [1] much nearer to my heart than any mere personal ambition of literary triumph was ever or will ever be. For fifteen years now I have been hoping against hope that the day might come when I should be able to pay the one due and sufficient tribute to the memory of the great man who in the last year of his long life was good enough to glorify me with the title of "his dear friend"—"let me," he wrote, "now and for ever call you so."

It is also very good natured of Mr. Ward to

[1] This looks as though Swinburne, after all, was to write the article on Landor in *The English Poets;* but there must have been a confusion in his mind about the matter, for Lord Houghton had agreed to deal with Landor, and tenaciously kept to his agreement. Mr. T. Humphry Ward, who had undertaken Collins, resigned that poet on hearing of Swinburne's desire.

make over Collins to me in such a graceful and courteous way. Pray let him know whenever you write how sincerely I appreciate it. Is this the same Prof. A. W. Ward who wrote a large and painstaking book on the English dramatists, good in other points but (especially as to Beaumont and Fletcher, Congreve and his comrades) terribly deformed and impaired by Puritanism?

You know how glad I shall be to see you any day you turn up. I want to discuss further my past proposal for a Critical Dictionary of the English Drama, to be undertaken by a company of us in common; and also to read you my last new poem of more than 400 lines—*On the Cliffs*. It is in the irregular Italian metre of *Lycidas*. Watts—as I possibly may have told you—says (what a man generally likes to hear of his latest work) that it is *the* best poem I ever wrote.[1] Come soon and see what you think of it.

Yours most sincerely,
A. C. SWINBURNE.

[1] It may be observed that Watts said this on every successive occasion.

LETTER XXVIII

To Lord Houghton

*The Pines,
Putney Hill,
S.W.*
November 21st, [1879].

[Swinburne has just received a letter from Lord Houghton, and is pleased that his new and permanent address "is known to others than duns."]

I keep no chambers in town henceforth, or (probably) for ever—finding after but too many years' trial that in the atmosphere of London I can never expect more than a fortnight, at best, of my usual health and strength. Here I am, like Mr. Tennyson at Farringford, close to the edge of a noble down, and I might add—

> Far out of sight, sound, smell of the town,

and yet within an easy hour's run of Hyde Park Corner, and a pleasant drive of Chelsea, where I have some friends lingering.

The first act of the third part of *Mary Stuart* has been some time in type; but there is no more yet in existence. I am going to publish early next year a small volume of verse now ready for the press, containing three poems, which range in length from upwards of 350 to 500 lines.[1]

You will see that in my forthcoming book on Shakespeare I have taken or made occasion, while speaking of him as a national or patriotic poet, to pay my tribute of almost passionate admiration to Tennyson's matchless and magnificent achievement in that line—the one great thing of its great kind done since Campbell, I mean, of course, his imperishable ballad on the death of Sir Richard Grenville—a poem as glorious as even the subject of it—*n'est ce pas?*

Have you seen the reprint (in a pretty form and limited number) of a rare if not unique pamphlet written in the thickest and hottest of the Reign of Terror, on novels and romances dealing with the tender passion in a modest elevated tone of feeling, which does infinite credit to the writer's own sweetness and amiable modesty of disposition—at such a season, too, for pastoral and domestic contemplations? The civic and sponsorial designation of this pure and gentle spirit was citizen Donatian-Alphonse-François ex-marquis de Sade.

How soothing it is for the philanthropic optimist to let his eye, weary of blood and horror, rest for a moment on the green and gushing oasis in a wilderness of crime, which is presented by the

---

[1] This was *Songs of the Springtides,* which was held back to include the Birthday Ode to Victor Hugo.

unhappily too rare existence of such (alas!) exceptional men!

> Ever yours truly,
> A. C. SWINBURNE.

LETTER XXIX

TO LORD HOUGHTON

> *The Pines,*
> *Putney Hill,*
> *S.W.*
> *November 27th,* [1879].

DEAR LORD HOUGHTON,
My attention and admiration are at present monopolized by Léon Cladel,[1] who makes me feel eighteen again in enthusiasm. I think some parts of *Bonshommes* are among the finest things I ever read for subtle truth and grim quaint pathos conveyed in a style whose perfection is beyond praise. And what a wonder for other qualities than its incomparable audacity and its exquisitely gorgeous attire and decorations is *Ompetrailles le Tombeau-des-Lutteurs!* It is a shame to speak first—perhaps to speak at all—of the outward splendours of a book (in the holy

[1] Léon Cladel (1835-92), an ultra-romantic disciple of Victor Hugo's prose. The two collections of stories mentioned in this letter were both quite recent when Swinburne wrote. Cladel's best book is *Les Va-nu-pieds* (1872).

Psalmist's phrase) "all glorious within"—but *when* will our hidebound hounds of publishers produce such a sample of choice ware? My two favourite *bits* (to use a word I hate) in text and illustration respectively are the faultless verbal photograph of the "Bourreau-des-Faubourgs" (pp. 262-265) in which the long since damned and rotten original who is now rotten and dead (thank Something) into the bargain lives and draws fetid and poisonous breath once more for one foul moment (but happily only on paper) and the admirable etching at p. 96 of "La Scorpione" in meditation ogling the—well, the muscles (let us say) of a Hercules. I think the amount of expression—of sombre and brooding lust, reflective and resolute appetite—which the etcher has put into her bent head is most masterly, and worthy even of the grim and savage seduction so wonderfully well given in the text.

When you have got the other book (if you have not got it, in which case excuse this officiously superfluous recommendation), mind you do as I did—read the story of "Dux" through at a single sitting without missing a word.

Passing from literature to life, I may tell you that I have begun housekeeping in common with a friend, on such terms that we can receive the ladies of our own respective families at any time, our household being at all points as respectable as the whitest of whited sepulchres. If either of us should ever want a change, he can go out without warning given or expected for a day (or night) or so. These (to speak Gampically) is our domestic arrangements and we find 'em answer.

Ever yours truly,
A. C. SWINBURNE.

LETTER XXX

TO EDMUND GOSSE

The Pines,
Putney Hill,
S.W.
December 16th, [1879].

MY DEAR GOSSE,
Many thanks for your Memoir of Rowlands,[1] which I have just received. I see you do not mention, what our friend Dr. Grosart might call the "mentionable" fact, that he once had the honour of being edited and commented on by no less a person than Sir Walter Scott, whose edition of *The Letting of Humour's Blood in the Head Vein* is in my possession. I quite agree with your

---

[1] This was the prefatory memoir prefixed to Mr. Gosse's edition of the works of Samuel Rowlands. *The Letting of Humour's Blood in the Head Vein* (1600) and *'Tis Merry when Gossips Meet* (1602) are two of the best of Rowland's satirical pamphlets.

favourable estimate of the *Gossips,* the only other thing I know of his.

I have just received and read *Alcilia*.[1] Is it not charming? I read out the two poems intervening to Watts, who is as enchanted as myself. I have written a word of warm thanks for it to Grosart, and congratulated him on the dedication of Breton.[2]

With best remembrances to Mrs. Gosse,
   Ever sincerely yours,
     A. C. SWINBURNE.

LETTER XXXI

To Lord Houghton

The Pines,
Putney Hill,
S.W.
December 22nd, [1879].

. . . Not six months back . . . I really was very ill for a time, tho' always conscious and

---

[1] *Alcilia: Philoparthen's Loving Pollie* (1595), an anonymous work reprinted by Grosart from a unique copy of the original discovered at Hamburg. Swinburne's admiration found expression in a sonnet, *The Resurrection of Alcilia* (*Studies in Song,* 1880).

[2] *The Works in Verse and Prose of Nicholas Breton,* edited, in two volumes, by A. B. Grosart, in 1879; with a "sonnet-dedicatory" to Mr. Gosse.

rational; je faisais de mauvais sang, et ne pouvais ni dormir ni digérer plusieurs semaines durant—je rendais tout, avec des vomissements jusqu'au sang—près. And I never was fresher or stronger or happier at twenty than now and for many weeks back . . . Nous enterrons bien tous les trois, je l'éspère, quelques centaines d'ignobles coquins . . .

I have today sent to the publishers a small MS. containing three poems[1] of the sea inscribed to the ancient monarch thereof—the Viking Trelawny, who has acknowledged the proposal of the dedication in a delightful note. There is just enough for a volume about as big (say) as Tennyson's or Browning's last.

Do you ever hear from Mrs. Proctor? I have not for ages,—and I remember she lives up a lift which is almost as impossible even for my fancy as to face a balloon. My head, I know, is remarkably good in any case of *natural* danger, but I draw the line at machinery. A man's courage, like his appetites, *ought* in my opinion to stop only—but to stop decisively—at the limit of natural and universal instinct, before we come (pace Mr. Gladstone) to Bulgary or balloons . . . That philobulgarious Christian's name reminds me of a ballad I wrote on Bright, Himself, and Carlyle, at the time of the B-g-rian horrescent agitation,

[1] *Songs of the Springtides.*

which if you behave pretty you may one day see, under the following Walter-Scotian title:—

The Quest of Sir Bright de Brummagem, Knight Templar: as it was recited on the Feast of Notre Dame des Bons Marchés, by a Perishing Savoyard:

A BALLAD OF BULGARY

I send you one stanza as a specimen of the Quaker's battle-cry.

> "*Strike, gentlemen, for sweet St. Penn!*
> *Up, gallants, for St. George;*
> *(His name in his day was Fox, by the way)*
> *Till the Paynim fiend disgorge.*"

As a good Mussulman, you are bound, irrespective of party, to share my contemptuous abhorrence of the Anglo-Russolators. What a song will I not write when Alexander the Liberator descends from the world!

Yours ever sincerely,
A. C. SWINBURNE

LETTER XXXII

To Auguste Vacquerie

*The Pines,
Putney Hill,
S.W.*
24 *mars* 1880.

CHER ET ILLUSTRE AMI,
   Merci deux fois des deux beaux volumes et de la bonne lettre que je viens de recevoir; merci, encore une fois, du noble journal où je pourrai suivre toujours avec intérèt et sympathie les developpements de votre cœur et de votre génie politique. A cet instant la politique en Angleterre prime tellement la littérature que les éditeurs osent à peine hasarder un livre d'imagination. Mais dans trois semaines il faut espérer que le public se remettra a lire autre chose que les journaux et alors il va sans dire que je vous ferai expédier un des premiers exemplaires de mes poésies nouvelles. En attendant, je vous serre la main de tout mon cœur.
                                    A. C. SWINBURNE.

[The MS. of this letter is now in the collection of Monsieur G. Jean-Aubry.]

LETTER XXXIII

TO LORD HOUGHTON

*The Pines,
Putney Hill,
S.W.
March 24th,* 1880.

DEAR LORD HOUGHTON,
I am glad you are writing on Landor as a poet. Besides *Gebir* and the *Hellenics*—of which all are good and some great—I rank among the highest works of his higher mood several of such shorter dramatic studies as "The Death of Anne Boleyn" and the Five Scenes on the Cenci story—of which D. G. Rossetti said once to me how far more lifelike and probable they had always seemed to him than Shelley's version. The interview between Beatrice and the Pope strikes me as worthy of almost any tragic poet. Another wonderful piece of work is that grim and glittering tragi-comedy in a nutshell called "The Coronation." Of his lyric, idyllic and elegiac masterpieces it would be almost an impertinence if I were to try and make out a list for you, whom I have sundry times heard repeat at greater length than I could the famous

lines against flower-gathering from his Faesulan Idyl.[1]

Yours ever,
A. C. SWINBURNE.

I met Mrs. Burton in town two days ago, in company with Landor's spiritual daughter (as he used to call her), Mrs. Lynn Linton. She is coming here to lunch in a few days.

LETTER XXXIV

To Lord Houghton

*The Pines,
Putney Hill,
S.W.
April 2nd, 1880.*

DEAR LORD HOUGHTON,
   I suppose of course you still include among your selections or citations from Landor the famous Hamadryad as first but one among the *Hellenics*. Is the Altar of Modesty too much "calculated to bring a blush to the cheek" of the

---

[1] *"I never pluck the rose; the violet's head
Hath shaken with my breath upon its bank
And not reproacht me; the ever-sacred cup
Of the pure lily hath between my hands
Felt safe, unsoiled, nor lost one grain of gold."*

virgin votaries of that goddess? I only ask for "information"—but I fear it must be, tho' certainly one of his most perfect pieces. In his very last years he retouched and altered it grievously for the worse, as I always thought, and Rossetti (to whom I once showed the new version, and who rates the original highest among Landor's poems) agreed with me. Acon and Rhodope, the original sequel to the Hamadryad, is a great favourite of mine—especially for its catalogue of wood-flowers—and why it was never reissued heaven only knows—if heaven ever took any heed of our poor glorious old friend's much entangled affairs. But of course the crown of all the Hellenics is the divine "Agamemnon and Iphigenia."

I have just made (ten minutes ago, in my cold bath) a version of his one only and noble Greek epigram—as follows:

Thy lifelong works, Napoleon, who shall write?
Time, in his children's blood who takes delight.

I doubt if he ever himself rendered anything more closely. I had tried at the couplet before, and given it up in despair. I have begun a Memorial Ode for his centenary—five years after date, but that shall not signify.

You promised me once a spare copy of his *Satyr on Satirists*—but I suppose since the fire you have none to spare. The copy you once gave me of his privately printed vindication *in re* Yescombe was destroyed in moving my papers by the (blank) negligence of packers. I would give much for another. I have almost as bad luck with his books as he had himself. I have lost my copies both of the *Last Fruit* and *Dry Sticks,* but I have his very first published volume of 1795, and all three editions of his Latin poems; also the *Gebir,* of 1803 in its quaint original green boards, wherein I take a bibliomaniacal delight.

Yours ever,
A. C. SWINBURNE.

[Mrs. Richard Burton, staying at the Pines, adds a note:—]

"I find Swinburne looking so well and cheerful, and we have been very merry. I wish you were here. Love to all.

"ISOBEL BURTON."

LETTER XXXV

TO EDMUND GOSSE

*The Pines,
Putney Hill,
S.W.
April 24th,* [1880].

MY DEAR GOSSE,

On Wednesday next, at 8 p.m. exactly, I am going to read some of my new poems [1] to a few friends. I hope you will be one of them. You know the way, but yet I may as well transcribe Watts's directions as to trains.

There are frequent trains direct from Waterloo on the S. W. line: also there is the Metropolitan, which has trains direct from Charing Cross at the hour and half hour. Should you come from the north side of London, by the Metropolitan, there are trains to Putney from High Street, Kensington, every half hour; and again, there is another set of trains from Gloucester Road to Putney every half hour.

With best regards to Mrs. Gosse, and my love and a kiss to the babies.

Ever yours,
A. C. SWINBURNE.

[1] The reading consisted of several long landscape poems, and a lyric called *Off Shore,* which Swinburne said he had written to prove that he could repeat the metrical effect of *Hertha.*

LETTER XXXVI

To Lord Morley

The Pines,
Putney Hill, S.W.
May 8th, 1880.

MY DEAR MORLEY,

Having fallen to at the glorious task you have done me the honour to set,[1] at six o'clock this morning, I think now in the evening I may with tolerable confidence undertake to send you the completed article—D. always V.—by the end (if not the middle) of this new-born week. Meantime I send you a lighter article thrown off a little while since without any idea of affixing my name to it; but when I consider that neither Diderot nor Voltaire would have felt nor would Hugo himself feel it a breach of dignity to set his heel publicly on such an ephemeral, I hardly see why I should stand more stiff on my dignity than they. You will see that of course there is no question of personal antagonism (God save the mark!) on my part. The subject, though fair game enough for any roving sportsman, would certainly not be worth my powder and shot, but for the momentary vogue of his

[1] A review of Victor Hugo's *Religions et Religion,* which appeared in *The Fortnightly Review* for June, 1880; first reprinted in *Les Fleurs du Mal and Other Studies*, 1913, pp. 39-55.

truly Christian impertinence—for which I fear (Something forgive me!) I, even I unwitting and unwary, may be in some degree innocently responsible. Having been carefully shewn only some parts, and those inoffensive enough, of the new Palissot's New Republic, I out of pure good-nature —one of the most perilous of human weaknesses or pernicious of human vices—recommended the book, on the strength of such passages as I had heard read aloud to my publisher. Pan forgive me, again—for thus I find myself in some small degree answerable for a whole following flood of effusive and orthodox impertinences poured out as fodder before the bovine public. Therefore if you will find or make room for this impromptu, it will gratify

Yours very sincerely,
A. C. SWINBURNE.

LETTER XXXVII

TO LORD MORLEY

*The Pines,
Putney Hill, S.W.
May 17, '80.*

MY DEAR MORLEY,

Your verdict on my article gives me genuine satisfaction. I thought it myself as good as time and space allowed. As to extracts, I most carefully examined the poem [1] with an eye to that possibility; and not without conviction that I should find sundry things fit for separate gathering; but ultimately & practically I c^d find none. Perhaps however the magnificent summary of truths necessary to salvation given at pp. 37, 38, under the heading "Chef d'œuvre" might serve as a sample of the "first manner" (to speak art-critically) of the poem—the passage (pp. 92–94) beginning "Matière ou pur esprit" and ending "contente des vers" of its second manner, in raillery of dogmatic materialism—and the conclusion, beginning at the last verse of p. 132, of the final part.

Copying would be impossible to me—I never could learn the art of transcription—and I always blunder. I used always to think it and I do now— the heaviest, brutallest, and stupidest of school punishments.

You must not think me "malè pertinacem"—like a Horatian young person's finger—if I plead for the epithets you mention. "Theophagous" is a simply and strictly accurate term of theological science (or nescience) and no whit stronger than phrases I remember in the controversial writings of orthodox Protestant divines, the latchets of whose shoes I am not—in a religious sense—worthy to unloose. "Christlike" (as opposed to Christian) I

---
[1] Hugo's *Religions et Religion*.

think at least as applicable to the author of *L'Art d'être Grandpère* as to any other secular admirer of the child-loving Socialist of Galilee whose human nature is so dear to Hugo: and there was a good deal more than "meekness and mildness" in the communistic field-preacher who was capable of a very gross and indefensible act of overt assault and battery on a set of respectable tradesmen trafficking in the shadow of the sanctuary by permission of the Dean and Chapter of Jerusalem. I, who am not generally impeached on the damning charge of meekness, content myself—as you may have seen—with a verbal assault on Dean Stanley for a very much graver offence.

As to Palissot the Little, I only want to have his castigation publicly carried into effect, and should naturally prefer the *Pall Mall* to the *Fortnightly Review* as a more fit and proper whipping-post for so small—as well as great—an offender. But of course I could not condescend to sign with my name *en toutes lettres* an "epistolary communication" on a subject of the sort:[1] tho' equally of course I should seek no disguise and desire no secrecy. If you think it worthy to appear under the modest signature of "Akakia fils," I shall be gratified. I do want to set my heel on the increasingly offensive little Christian creature without doing him the honour of too much notice—especially as (*mea*

[1] No such "epistolary communication" has been traced.

maxima culpa!) I unwarily helped to bring him forward and gave him occasion to sting my heel—or try to sting it.

                Yours very sincerely,
                      A. C. SWINBURNE.

LETTER XXXVIII

TO EDMUND GOSSE

The Pines,
July 8th, 1880.

MY DEAR GOSSE,

I am not "wroth" with your editorial friends:[1] but I certainly thought and think—Watts also thought and thinks with me—that it was unjustifiably unfair to garble my note by suppression—not of any strong language or objectionable allusions, but of the evidence adduced that the character and conduct of my assailant were such as to make all further controversy impossible on my part. I was also surprised to find that while a leading and separate place had been assigned to the attack, which was duly registered in the weekly table of contents, the mutilated fragment of my reply was smuggled into so obscure a corner that

[1] Mr. James Sutherland Cotton, the Editor of *The Academy*. All this refers to continued disputation with Furnivall; the quarrel was beginning to bore the public.

for some time I thought it had simply been suppressed. I am not in the least surprised (tho' Watts says *he* is, considering what *was* allowed to appear) to learn that it was requisite to suppress much of Furnivall's letter as unfit for publication. Whenever Thersites Minor opens his lips, I am aware that they are "not words alone" which drop thence. What they are I shall not specify: but, as Horatio remarks to Hamlet, I most assuredly "might have rhymed."

God knows how sick I am of the dirty little subject: but from one point of view it is really of no small or merely private importance. We are wont to boast that in point of literary manners we have got far ahead of the days of *The Dunciad*. It is full time for us to look well to it that we do not fall far behind them. This is neither the first nor the tenth nor the twentieth time that I have had to remark how far worse than in the worst days of the past would be such a condition of letters as seems really and rapidly to be coming upon us; when every liberty is conceded to every blackguard whose unwashed fingers will not shrink from grasping it, and every gate of retaliation or chastisement is closed against every man of other than the blackguard's breed.

I know that I am very far from being the only person, or the worthiest of attention, who thinks this a matter to be most heedfully weighed and seen to. Never yet has English literature been so damnably degraded, as most inevitably and most deservedly it must and will be, if such fellows as this "mordiloquent menial" are to discharge themselves in public without fear of whipping. No one of nicer stomach than Swift or Pope would undertake the scavenger's rather than hangman's office of stripping them: but their beastly license will make the paths of literature impassable and improper for the decent feet of cleanly people, if such are forbidden even to point in passing at the naked nastiness of their self-exposure.

You will oblige—not me, but (what is rather more important) all men who have any care for the interest and dignity of English letters, if you can prevail upon the editor of such a paper as *The Academy* to lay this matter seriously to heart. It is of very much less importance whether or not he does himself and me the justice which I think he should do of printing my short and studiously reticent note of two days since, in which I briefly and finally indicated the systematic and consistent misrepresentation of my real argument, and evasion of its main point, by my would-be antagonist. And, this done, I think that outside the publications of the Sham Shaxpere Society the question should be considered as finally closed. *Paulò majora*—and above all *paulò dulciora*. (Watts has read and cordially agrees with every word of the above.)

I have enough stock ready for another verse-book in the autumn. There is one poem [1] in seven parts, just a little longer than *Thalassius,* which Watts likes better than anything I ever did (and in metrical and antiphonal effect I prefer it myself to all my others) : so I shall inscribe it to him.

Come soon and hear it. There are two more finished which you have not seen, and one incomplete. *The Song for the Centenary of Landor* five years since sums up what I have to say of my great old friend on all accounts whether critical or personal—and I know how much he would have preferred to have it said in verse, the best that I could command—which I have certainly done all I can to give him, and to make as nearly worthy of him as may be—wishing earnestly that it were nearer that inaccessible mark of worthiness. But the limit of eight hundred lines is pitifully narrow for such a Titanic charge as the panegyric of such a Titan.[2]

Ever yours sincerely,
A. C. SWINBURNE.

[1] *By the North Sea* (*Studies in Song*).

[2] *Studies in Song,* the volume announced in this letter, was not ready "in the autumn," but was published in January, 1881, though the date on the title is 1880.

LETTER XXXIX

To Lord Morley

*The Pines,
    Putney Hill, S.W.
    Sept. 19th, 1880.*

MY DEAR MORLEY,

Having just finished my revision of the revised proof which I received yesterday,[1] I write to ask if you would like to have for the next month's number a paper on English poetry[2] of an earlier date than that of the present subject—or subjects: a short summary of flying notes on the general view which presents itself to me (1) of Chaucer, especially in his relation to the two other members of the mediæval trinity—in (anything rather than) unity—of great poets representing three different countries & three diverse classes: Dante, aristocracy & Italy; Chaucer, the British bourgeoisie or English middle class; Villon, France and the mediæval "prolétariat"; and each characteristically for better and for worse, for greater and for smaller qualities: (2) of Spenser, and (3) of Shakespeare's sonnets—all these of course in the merest outline, but

---

[1] *Sed Vide* P.S. [A.C.S.]
[2] *Short Notes on English Poets,* printed in *The Fortnightly Review* for December 1880, and reprinted in *Miscellanies,* 1886, pp. 1-24.

of course as accurate and full as I can make the said outline within the limits of a sketch: (4) of Milton, with special reference (*a*) to *Samson Agonistes* which I have often been (unfashionably and heretically) inclined to put, on the whole, at the head of all his works—(*b*) to his relation towards Cromwell and the Commonwealth—and (*c*) to his personal polemics, on which Mr. Pattison has borne so heavily. But you will see that all these matters are handled only in the most rapid way of suggestion, with hints and remarks thrown out literally *au courant de la plume,* when you hear that the whole essay or study is not so long by two or three pages as the one you have in the forthcoming number.

Yours very truly,
A. C. Swinburne.

P.S.—As you see, I kept this back for a time on second thoughts, and have since made a few revisions and additions in the essay, but, for the rest, this note may stand as it was written.

A. C. S., Oct. 3d.

If ever you *do* come to look me up, I can—*à propos de Milton*—shew you some fine "first editions." But I forget whether or not you are bitten with bibliomania.

LETTER XL

To Edmund Gosse

*The Pines,
Putney Hill,
S.W.
November 18th,* [1880].

MY DEAR GOSSE,
 I had already heard with much pleasure of your projected book of select odes.[1] I congratulate you on the prospect of so noble and delightful a task. But I should not like—indeed I should rather object—to be represented by so merely occasional a piece as the Candiote Ode [2]— literally, almost, an impromptu, having thrown off on the occasion *au courant de la plume,* I think in two sittings: and being in my opinion—except perhaps the *Epode,* which is a little better than the rest—altogether a palpably hasty and comparatively inferior piece of work. Watts thinks—and I with him—most decidedly that my representative ode is *The Eve of Revolution;* which accordingly I should be happy to place at your service, and to see in such good company. The other would be— *me judice*—a very poor finish, a veritable anti-

[1] *English Odes* (Kegan Paul & Co., 1881).
[2] *Ode on the Insurrection in Candia,* from *Songs before Sunrise.*

climax, to a worthy collection of English odes. I am impatient to see the book, and feel really honoured by your intention of closing it with the name of

    Yours very sincerely,
      A. C. SWINBURNE.

When will you come to get a foretaste of my forthcoming poems?[1] It must be soon, for the printers have the last revised proofs in hand.

LETTER XLI

TO EDMUND GOSSE

The Pines,
Putney Hill,
S.W.
November 20th, 1880.

MY DEAR GOSSE,
  To begin with the more important subject of your note—I admire some verses of the *Ode to Miletus* as much as any one, but certainly would not choose it as *the* sample of Landor. That *To Joseph Ablett* seems to me altogether the finest and fittest for selection [2]—tho' there are noble verses in those to Southey and Wordsworth. But the *Ode to*

---

[1] *Studies in Song.*
[2] In accordance with Swinburne's advice, the *Ode to Joseph Ablett* was chosen to represent Landor, and the Coleridge couplet was replaced.

Ablett has at once the most of lyric or poetic beauty, and the most of personal character and charm. I hope you will agree with me on this point, after collation of the poems. See also Forster's excellent commentary on the ode in question—and mind you replace (supposing you take my advice as to choice of poem) the beautiful couplet on the death of Coleridge, which Forster there supplies, afterwards cancelled in some spleenful mood.

As to my own lyrics, I must reiterate that I would rather "shine by my absence" than be represented by the Candiote impromptu. As the best of my odes is too long for your purpose (it is exactly a hundred lines shorter than one of Pindar's), the address in *Poems and Ballads* "to Victor Hugo in Exile" (these two last words ought now be added to the title) would perhaps suit better. It is as much of an ode in form as Milton's *On the Nativity*.

     Yours very sincerely,
      A. C. SWINBURNE.

LETTER XLII

To Edmund Gosse

*The Pines,
Putney Hill,
S.W.
December 3rd,* 1880.

My dear Gosse,
Of course the right reading is *his*—not *this* (!!!!) world. Those predestinate sons of Tophet, the printers, seem to have reduced my text to the condition of a "later quarto"—worthless—with new corrupt readings added to those of the "first quarto" (*vide* editorial notes on old plays *passim*). May the Supreme Being judge and condemn their sanguinary spirits.

I think my ode [1] was written the year before it appeared—*i.e.*, in '65—or possibly in '64, but I think not. I have never registered and ticketed my poems chronologically after the characteristic fashion of Wordsworth. I only know that I was already in correspondence with the Master. The first letter I ever received from him was in the summer of '62—more than eighteen years gone, and yet we have never shaken hands. It is written in acknowledgment—very far too kindly expressed—

[1] *To Victor Hugo.*

of some crude and over-bold articles (not signed) on *Les Misérables,* which he had actually been at the trouble to trace to my hand by inquiry after the author's name. In my reply I asked leave to inscribe *Chastelard*—then in the course of composition—to him: and when it appeared three years later, he expressed himself in very warm terms of gratification as to the language of the inscription. It was then still the habit of *The Times* and all the rest of the great or little vermin of English journalism seldom to mention his name—as far as I ever saw—without insult and ridicule. *The Saturday Review* on *Les Contemplations* was a notable exception—followed later (*mirabile dictu*) by *The Quarterly* on *Les Misérables.*

Yours very sincerely,
A. C. SWINBURNE.

LETTER XLIII

To Lord Houghton

<i>The Pines,
Putney Hill, S.W.
December 18th,</i> 1880.

DEAR LORD HOUGHTON,

Though you did not encourage my design, when I told you of it on your last visit here, of a memorial poem on Landor, I feel none the less bound in common gratitude to send the first copy I send to any one of the book which contains it, to the man whose kindness procured me the great honour and delight of being received as a friend by one of the three great men who seemed to me as a schoolboy the three above all others whom I should most like, when a man, to do homage to. To Mazzini Karl Blind introduced me: to Victor Hugo some very boyish articles of my own seemed enough to make me worthy of his notice: but I owe it to you that Landor ever honoured me with the name of "his dear friend": I wish I had something worthier to send in proof of gratitude to you and reverence for him.

Do you know the "dead cathedral city" which I have tried to describe in the last poem in this book, Dunwich in Suffolk? The whole picture is from life—salt marshes, ruins and bones protruding seawards through the soil of the crumbling sandbanks.

What a divine and transcendent poem is Tennyson's "Rizpah"! But you will see what I think of it,—if you care to look into the *Fortnightly*,—in ten days' time.[1]

Ever yours truly,
A. C. SWINBURNE.

My book is not yet published—so that I give you the maidenhead of my latest child.

[1] *Tennyson and Musset, Fortnightly Review*, February, 1881.

LETTER XLIV

To RICHARD HERNE SHEPHERD

*The Pines,
Putney Hill.
December* 24th, 1880.

Dear Sir,
Pray accept my sincere thanks for your very handsome present,[1] which I have begun to examine—with what interest you will see when I tell you that I suspect—though it is mere suspicion—that you have not exhausted the list of Thackeray's contributions to *Fraser*. When an undergraduate, I looked up some of these in the Union Library, and detected in a review (for instance) either of the pictures of the year (about '38) or of its illustrated books, a well-known passage in *Vanity Fair*—where it appeared some ten years later. And just before *Catherine* appeared another burlesque or grotesque horror—*Elizabeth Brownrigge,* a story in two parts, which ought to be Thackeray's, for, if it is not, he stole the idea, and to some extent the style, of his parodies on novels of criminal life, from this first sketch of the kind.

Yours very truly,
A. C. SWINBURNE.

[1] *The Bibliography of Thackeray.*

LETTER XLV

To Lord Morley

> The Pines,
> Putney Hill, S.W.
> Feb. 6th, '81.

My dear Morley,
    One line to acknowledge with thanks the cheque with a note dated Feb. 1st.

When I bring down my desultory but progressive "Studies in English Poetry" to this century, I shall have more to say on Byron than is said in the article of which Mr. Arnold speaks so kindly.[1] I should much like to know what was the sentence which found such favour in his sight for what the illustrious enemy whom we all lament would have called its Veracity. But nothing will ever supplant—even if one or two suggestions may here and there correct or modify in detail—the final and admirable estimate given in Nichol's book.

> Yours sincerely,
> A. C. Swinburne.

I have just had a really delightful letter of much more than compliment from Browning, on my vo-

---

[1] Swinburne's Prefatory Essay to *A Selection from the Works of Lord Byron*, 1866.

tive poem to Landor;[1] and I am not even yet old enough not to be gratified by cordiality of the kind from my elders. I hope he does not think himself disparaged by the comparison with Leconte de Lisle.

LETTER XLVI

To Edmund Gosse

*The Pines,
Putney Hill,
S.W.
March 1st, 1881.*

My dear Gosse,
 A thousand thanks for the gift of your masterly and most interesting study of Etheredge.[2] I had already read it, having of course sent (on its account) for the number as soon as ever I saw the contents announced—and read it, I need not say, with equal attention and enjoyment. It is just twenty years since I made Sir George's—and Sir Fopling's—acquaintance. I have always placed him far away at the head of the Restoration dramatists, equally above "hasty Shadwell and slow Wycherly," whom when Rochester promoted to

[1] *Song for the Centenary of Walter Savage Landor,* printed in *Studies in Song,* 1880, pp. 1-65.
[2] Sir George Etheredge (1635?-1691), the dramatist, who had up to that time been entirely neglected. His works were not edited until 1888.

share the first place he must have been not merely as malignant as usual but considerably stupider. Not, of course, that both are not excellent in their way.

I know nothing but should like to know more of your friend Wilson.[1] But what do *you* not know of the literature of that always amusing and interesting period—and indeed of our national drama in all its seasons? And once I thought myself rather learned—I blush to remember it—in that line! But it was before I knew you.

I have mislaid (as usual) the address of the Editor of *The Encyclopædia Britannica.* I believe you are a contributor—can you send it me? for till I have it I cannot send *him* my article on Keats, which has lain ready these many days. I should like to show it to you before it goes, if you could find an hour or two to come and talk it over.

May we not hope that this article is but the forerunner of *The Life and Works of Sir G. Etheredge, now first etc. etc.?* You could hardly do a greater service—at least in that way—to English Letters. In the meantime Watts particularly desires me not to forget to let you know how thoroughly he shares my admiration of the good work

---

[1] John Wilson (1627?-1696), the author of *The Cheats* and *The Projectors.*

already done by your article, which he read with even as hearty interest and enjoyment as my own.
Ever sincerely yours,
A. C. SWINBURNE.

P.S.—I reopen this to ask if you feel sure about Dryden's words meaning that Etheredge was fifty-one at the time of their metrical correspondence. Of course I knew the verses well enough, but always had thought—blunderingly, I daresay—that they meant "by coming thither from—and so bringing with you the temperature of—two degrees higher latitude"—but, I repeat, I daresay this is sheer ignorance.

LETTER XLVII

To Edmund Gosse

The Pines,
April 7th, 1881.

MY DEAR GOSSE,
I must lose no time in thanking you for the exquisite little book [1] which arrived last night —a flower or a jewel of a song-book. I am proud to be found worthy of the last place in it—and amused to see who is my next neighbour,[2] and

[1] *English Odes,* 1881.
[2] Coventry Patmore.

what are his ideas of lyric style and the structure of an ode. I think you have been rather cruel to the Laureate: it was hard on him to reprint two such pieces as you have given: but perhaps the man who could be capable of writing either may be said to deserve that neither should be charitably forgotten.

I think your favourite Cowley might have been better represented. Is not his *Ode to Brutus* a finer sample of his better style than these? To my mind also there is too much of Gray: but I should say that, despite my respect for Matthew Arnold's opinion, I am a heretic—and always have been—as to *The Progress of Poesy,* about which I am rather disposed to agree with Dr. Samuel Johnson.

Watts and I are both deeply shocked at the audacious indecency of the opening lines of Warton's *Ode to Spring!* How can anyone have the effrontery to put a volume containing a picture so improper into female hands? Is this the result of too much devotion to such writers as Etheredge? I blush alike for the author and the editor. Aphra Behn might have been ashamed of it.

To be serious again for a moment—you must let me say how very much I regret that you should have thought fit, in such a place as you have chosen, to tax Landor with "splenetic caprice" in the suppression of his couplet on Coleridge. I have little doubt that his reason was one equally just and simple: such an estimate—unhappily, in my opinion, inevitable by any reasonable man—of Coleridge's personal character as compelled him, under pain of insincerity and a conscious touch of the absurd, to rescind his letters of beatification.

I have completed about a quarter or so of an Ode addressed to the Greeks,[1] which I hope and expect will be worthier of the subject than that on the rising in Crete.

Ever sincerely yours,
A. C. SWINBURNE.

P.S.—Your note has just arrived (10 a.m.) before I had sent off this letter. Watts desires me to give you his kind thanks for your message, and to say that he has been very ill (which is too true—with a "whoreson cold, sir; a cough, sir"—like Falstaff's recruit) but is now really getting better, though as yet still confined to the house.

[1] *Athens: An Ode,* printed in *Tristram of Lyonesse and Other Poems,* 1882, pp. 171-179.

LETTER XLVIII

To Sir Sidney Colvin

The Pines,
Putney Hill,
S.W.
May 24th, 1881.

My dear Colvin,
   Nothing could give me more satisfaction than to be of any service as an auxiliary in any work undertaken to do honour to the memory of Landor. Of course you are acquainted with Mrs. Lynn Linton's two admirable articles in *Fraser*? I have as usual forgotten where I have stowed away the numbers, and have just spent a fruitless hour in hunting them through sundry dusty paper-heaps that I might send you the date for reference in case you too should have mislaid or forgotten the most valuable and I am convinced (as far as it goes) the trustworthiest account of Landor in existence. They were written rather by way of correction than of supplement to Forster's far worse than inadequate picture of the old lion. I have myself been quite recently busied in condensing the same ninety years into the compass (not even of a small book, but) of a biographical and critical article for the *Encyclopædia Britannica* which the editor to my great satisfaction has accepted without demur

either as to its length or as to its enthusiasm. It is more than improbable, I ought however to say, that I should be able to supply you with any fact or correct for you any error unsupplied or uncorrected by such authority as that of Mr. Browning. I am eager to see the book, and shall expect to find in it not merely "a point or two" but many points of interest new to me.

The oddest thing about Forster—who certainly was not a malevolent but really a well intentioned man—is the excellent quality of his work as a biographer of men whom he had never seen, when contrasted with the execrable—a clergyman might say, damnable—quality of his work as a biographer of men whom he knew personally.

Believe me,
Yours sincerely,
A. C. SWINBURNE.

P.S.—I have copies of Landor's two first publications, the book and the anonymous pamphlet of 1795. Of course I could not let them out of my hands, but if you never saw and wish to see them I shall be glad to show them to you. They are full of curious interest.

P.P.P.S.—I do most earnestly hope that you will find room—as Forster did not—for the text of Landor's prose palinode on Byron (*Imaginary Conversations,* 1st series, "the second edition, corrected and enlarged," 1826: vol. 1, pp. 220–221), I know nothing nobler as prose writing, nothing quite so noble as an evidence of character, in all the range of letters. Part of it was afterwards recast, worked into a different form and set in a new frame, but the first words on Byron's death—"written as if in star-fire and immortal tears"—are the best. If you cannot conveniently refer to that particular edition, I will copy out for you the whole note on condition that you insert it. It will be the best page in a good book if you do.

June 2nd.—I find a fresh instalment of your proofs on the breakfast table just as I was about to despatch this letter. The 1st (Oxford) edition of Idyllia (v. p. 90) certainly did see the light, as I have picked up two copies of it myself. One of these I gave to the Master of Balliol, he was so delighted with the book—one of the most exquisitely printed little square volumes I ever saw, *"Idyllia nova quinque Heroum atque Heroidum,"* etc.

>   Ἡμεις δε πονους, οὑς εκ παιδος
>   Μοχθουμεν αει   .   .   .
>   .   .   .   Πτηνων τ'αγελας
>   [1]Ἀ βλαπτουσιν
>   Σεμν' αναθηματα, τοξοισιν εμοις
>   Φυγαδος θησομεν   Eurip., *Ion.*

[1] It is A in the folio Cambridge edition of 1694, which Landor may have used. It should of course be Αἲ as Swinburne points out.

(No accents in the Greek motto—is it not a happy one?)

Date 1815, dedicated in an epistle thus addressed: "Savagius Landor doctissimo atque optimo viro. S. Parr, S.P.D." The second division of the book is headed "Nemesis sive Improborum Poenae."

I must add a beautifully Landorian note at the end of the preface: "Pauca libet subjicere. Si quid lucelli reportaverit domum librarius, id jussu meo dabit Lipsiensibus, immeritâ laborantibus paupertate. Atqui vix ausim sperare fore ut apud eum postulentur haec cc exemplaria me vivente!"

The five Idyls are Corythus, Dryope, Pan et Pitys, Coresus et Callirhoë, Helena ad Pudoris Aram. Then follow Iambi et Hendecasyllabi, eight in number, two whole poems out of these devoted to Lawyer Launton: then Elegiae, three of them; then four detached poems, all (I think) afterwards reproduced.

Since I wrote the third postscript of this straggling letter, I have read what you say at p. 94 *in re* Byron *v.* Landor: it is of course there that it would give me such delight if you could insert Landor's magnificent tribute to Byron when newly dead.

[It looks as though the second postscript were missing from the letter, as presented to the Fitzwilliam Museum by Sir Sidney Colvin in 1912.]

LETTER XLIX

To Sir Sidney Colvin

> The Pines,
> Putney Hill,
> S.W.
> June 1st, 1881.

My dear Colvin,
 The *Italics* I have somewhere with sundry other waifs and strays mostly in the form of flysheets, English and Latin. The entire text of the said *Italics,* if I do not mistake (as I am confident I do not), was incorporated into *The last Fruit off an old Tree.* The *Simonidea* I never saw. The name I think is entered (? in MS.) in the *old* catalogue of the British Museum, where I vainly tried to get at the book. But I never heard of its being so combustible a bit of ware as you intimate. On reference to both editions of Forster I can find nothing which implies, much less which asserts, that the author took any pains to suppress it. I doubt very much whether Byron's allusion to the "edifying Ithyphallics" was aimed at a pamphlet printed so long before; especially as the Italian edition of the "Idyllia" had appeared in 1820. The Byronic reference is rather, I think, to the hendecasyllabic lines "Ad Mulum" where the very word "ithyphallics" occurs in a line afterwards cancelled

—not unreasonably. And—which is more important, and to me conclusive—Landor in 1847 distinctly asserted that he had in the edition of that year allowed all the poems impugned to stand in disproof or rather in defiance of the impeachment. "Vituperavit aliquis ludicra liberiùs in juventute scripta. *Quantula sint hæc et quàm paucula nunc videbis.* Facile esset a novis chartis delere quae tamen detrectantium memoria non remittit; atqui vix operae pretium est, *et ingenuo minùs convenit."—Ad Robertum fratrem* ("Poem. et Inscr.," p. 350).

I hope you mean to give at least a word in passing to the said Robert's admirable plays. None of Walter's are nearly so well constructed or of such sustained interest in action and development as "The Earl of Brecon" and "The Ferryman"; and they are so equally noble in manner and matter! There is a slip at p. 36; the *Poems from the Arabic and Persian* were reprinted (with an explanatory note) in the luckless volume of Dry Sticks. Some "demi-devil" has robbed me of that book and also of a copy cherished since my schoolboyhood of the *Last Fruit.* I have also lost—it was destroyed in "two removes as bad as a fire"—a copy given me by Lord Houghton of Mr. Landor's *Vindication* (or *Explanation*; I forget which; but you should by all means look it up) printed, but impossible to get published, after the wretched Yescombe business, containing *inter alia* a letter from the father of the young lady whose name was mixed up in it, earnestly and cordially thanking Landor for his great services in rescuing and restoring to him his daughter, who by Landor's persuasion had left the respectable clerical couple whose company she had preferred to home, and returned safe to her own family, thanks only to his good and wise advice. An enthusiastic little word of grand-daughterly gratitude was added from the truant girl herself. I suppose you could not even yet make full use of this pamphlet, which is certainly not written throughout in rosewater; but (as you probably know from inspection) it is simply unanswerable as a vindication of the glorious old man's character from any charge but one (which it assuredly does not tend to disprove) of excess in generosity, credulity, enthusiasm of open-handed charity and open-hearted—alas! also open-mouthed indignation. I am not sure about Mrs. Linton's *second* article. I suspect it was an error of mine. With most cordial congratulations on the excellent success of your great and laborious undertaking (as far as I have seen),

Yours sincerely,
A. C. SWINBURNE.

P.S.—Can any *Phocaeans* (to me unknown) be more incomprehensible than *Chrysaor?* No brother Landorite (to be sure there are not many of us) could ever unriddle for me that passage about "Atrobal." I find nothing to "correct"—much to interest in your remarks on the unpublished verses concerning the lovely name of Ianthe.

P.P.S.—Excuse this exceptionally awful scrawl—almost as bad as Landor's own—the only point on which I can hope to rival him in writing—if even there he can ever be rivalled—except by Shakespeare.

LETTER L

To John Churton Collins

*The Pines,
Putney Hill,
S.W.
June 28th,* 1881.

My dear Collins,

Many thanks for your exquisite edition of Lord Herbert. I had been looking for many days with an envious and an evil eye on the copy sent to Watts, and this comes in good time to exorcise the devil which tempted me to break the tenth commandment.

How lovely in feeling, and how near excellence in expression, is the madrigal at p. 25.

Will you not come over some of these hot bright

days and hear some of my latest poems? The principal, on Athens,[1] is thought one of my best by the friends whose judgment I most value: and there are enough others for a volume. But it seems my last [2] have not sold well enough to encourage the delusion that *The Spectator* may not be right in its assertion that the British purchaser has begun once for all to see through the hollow emptiness of my pretensions.

Ever sincerely yours,
A. C. SWINBURNE.

LETTER LI

To Lord Morley

The Pines,
Putney Hill, S.W.
Nov. 24, '81.

My dear Morley,

The same hour that I revised the proof [3] I returned it to the printer with corrections. I trust in the God of Tennyson it has not miscarried. The characteristic and necessary *dashes* indicating the breaks and pauses of passion or anguish were

[1] Written in April, 1881, and included in the *Tristram* volume of 1882.

[2] *Songs of the Springtides*, 1880.

[3] The proof of *Disgust, a Dramatic Monologue*, printed in *The Fortnightly Review* for December 1881, and reprinted in *Posthumous Poems*, 1910, pp. 187-192.

shamefully often omitted, to the injury at once of panting metre and of gasping sense. Even the last pathetic words—"But anyhow—there—I won't" were reduced (strange to say) to mere nonsense by the omission of the second dash and made to run thus—"—there I won't"—which it w^d have driven the author mad to see published.

Don't you think Sala owes me a return puff for my reference to the immortal Quagg?

You shall have the essay on Mary[1] in a day or two. Shall I send it to Berkeley Lodge, or to Spottiswoode & Co. at once?

Ever yours,
A. C. SWINBURNE.

LETTER LII

To Lord Morley

*The Pines,
Putney Hill,
S.W.
December 11th, 1881.*

MY DEAR MORLEY,

I hope my request for a revise of the proof of my essay on Mary,[2] with the first proof

---

[1] *Note on the Character of Mary Queen of Scots,* printed in *The Fortnightly Review* for January 1882, and reprinted in *Miscellanies,* 1886, pp. 373-390.

[2] *Note on the Character of Mary Queen of Scots, printed in The Fortnightly Review* for January, 1882.

returned for collation, will not interfere with its place in the *January* number. I could wish the proof had come a little earlier than last night, as there are some troublesome blunders which require a revision, and are not, I must say, on collation of proof and MS., explicable by any carelessness in the MS.—two words interpolated in one place (the words "to be"), which simply turn a sentence of tolerably good into one of intolerably bad literary style—and two notes of capital importance misplaced, in the face of a perfectly clear MS. direction, so as to produce an effect of most bewildering nonsense.

To the friend rather than the editor I venture to expose my satisfaction at one result already obtained by my latest book [1]—and I hope you will not think me the vainest of men and most obtrusive of egoists, if I cannot refrain from telling you what a letter I have received from the one English poet living for whose opinion as an authority on poetic drama I care a cracked farthing—"I have named," of course, the author of *Philip van Artevelde,* who has written me seven pages of the kindest and most gratifying acknowledgment that ever a poet on the verge of eighty-two wrote to a younger labourer in the same field.

Would anything but ocular evidence have made one believe that there were two men on the re-

[1] *Mary Stuart: a Tragedy,* 1881.

viewing press who would undertake to write on the subject of my play in ignorance of Lady Shrewsbury's famous "scandal about Queen Elizabeth" retailed to her by "dear sister" Mary with such unctuous relish in a letter which Froude, Hozack, nay, Miss Strickland, mention or cite or transcribe at length? And here now is *The Academy* following suit after *The Saturday Review* in the display of utter ignorance that ever such a letter was written! These be thy prophets, O Culture! Though you would not print my little word on the certainly very paltry subject, I have hit on a way of gibbeting the more impertinent Dunce of the two by means of capital letters in advertising columns.

Ever yours,
A. C. SWINBURNE.

P.S.—I had all but forgotten the most important thing I had to say. Would there be any difficulty in my causing to be printed at once a few copies of my *Note on the character of Mary Q. of S.* for strictly private distribution—none, of course, for sale?[1]

[1] This project, for some unknown reason, was not carried out.

LETTER LIII

To John Churton Collins

> The Pines,
> Putney Hill,
> S.W.
> Wednesday, [1882].

My dear Collins,

Can you come at such short notice to a swarry consisting of recitations from a forthcoming poem, and subsequent supper, on Friday? Do if you can, and (as Mrs. Jarley says) "be in time," eight sharp. I have been busier of late than ever before in my life, between the correction of proofs for the biggest book of verse [1] (bar *Bothwell*) I ever put forth, and the compilation of a life of Mary Queen of Scots for the *Encyclopædia Britannica*. I am greatly set up by the compliment of being chosen for that office above all the historians and other prose folk whose services might have been secured, and their authority preferred, to that of a mere poet like

Yours very sincerely,
A. C. SWINBURNE.

[1] *Tristram of Lyonesse and Other Poems,* published in July, 1882.

LETTER LIV

To Edmund Gosse

The Pines,
January 5th, '81 (sic) [1882].

MY DEAR GOSSE,
I ought to have answered your question before now, but your note was mislaid. Gray's travelling companion must have been an ancestress of mine; but on applying to the oldest living member of the family nothing further illustrative of her character could be discovered. There was then living a *Mrs.* Swinburne,[1] wife of a younger brother (the so-called "traveller" and sole author produced by the family till our own degenerate days), who has left a tradition of character answering to Gray's description. This is all the explanation I could get last year, when I happened to come

[1] In October, 1753, Gray travelled from York to Stilton with "a Lady Swinburne, a Roman Catholick, not young, that had been much abroad, seen a great deal, knew a great many people, very chatty and communicative, so that I passed my time [for three days] very well." This was Mary Bedingfeld, who had married Sir John Swinburne, the 3rd baronet, in 1721. She was the mother of Henry Swinburne (1743-1803), the "so-called traveller," and the poet was her lineal descendant. From letters still unpublished in the care of the Bedingfeld family, it appears that she continued her acquaintance with Gray, and invited him to visit her at York. She died in 1761.

upon the passage in Gray's letters myself, and applied for elucidation or illustration to the proper quarter.

With all seasonable good wishes for you and yours,

Believe me ever,
Yours sincerely,
A. C. SWINBURNE.

LETTER LV

To E. C. Stedman

The Pines,
Putney Hill,
S.W.
April 4th, 1882.

MY DEAR MR. STEDMAN,

It is a real gratification to see your friendly handwriting again. If ever I come to America yours will probably be about the first address to which I shall betake myself. For the last two years I have been stronger and harder at work—the only test of strength and happiness for some temperaments—than ever I was in my life that I remember. The above is my standing address; where, though within a postal district (as you see) of London, I am practically in the country, on the verge of a great moor or down, and within an easy walk of some of the loveliest woodland and meadow scenery in England. I hope my next account received of you may assure me that your own health and spirits are duly restored.

Mary Stuart has found no favour with the reading or reviewing public, but has procured me two satisfactions (I doubt Landor would never have permitted me the use of such a plural), which I prefer infinitely to six columns of adulation in *The Times* and any profit thence resulting. (1) A letter from the venerable and revered father— in age—of all living English (or other) poets, in which the illustrious author [1] of *Philip van Artevelde* bestows such nobly cordial and unreserved praise on the play as I must not transcribe, but should like to show you. (2) An application from the editor of the *Encyclopædia Britannica*—who might, I suppose, in Macaulay's time, almost command the services of the most eminent scholars and historians of the country—to me, a mere poet, proposing that I should contribute to that great repository of erudition the biography of Mary Queen of Scots. I doubt if the like compliment was ever paid before to one of our "idle trade!" To this task I am about to set myself as soon as I have finished my long narrative poem in nine parts—

[1] Sir Henry Taylor. See *Letters from A. C. Swinburne to Sir Henry Taylor and Other Correspondents*, 8vo, 1912.

Tristram of Lyonesse. I am now engaged on the last canto, or book, or whatever the reader may choose to call it.

My next volume, which will go to the press as soon as this main *pièce de résistance* is ready to be served up, will contain, besides, upwards of fifty lyrical poems—mostly, of course, short; and the greater number of them studies of childhood or songs about children—and various odes and sonnets on literary, historic, and political matters; among them a series of twenty-one sonnets on the English dramatic poets from 1590 to 1650, which I hope will interest those who share my devotion to that branch of our older poetry, and perhaps attract to the study of it some who have not yet embarked on that most delightful and inexhaustible line of reading, which is to me (as far as enjoyment goes) all that ever it was to Charles Lamb. In that case I shall certainly have been of some service in my generation.

Thanks for the little notice on my play. The only good one I have seen (with one Italian exception) is the work of a Russian, written in French (in Russ it would not have edified me). I shall look out for your article on Mr. Lowell, whose acquaintance I had the pleasure of making not long since (a very real pleasure it was to me), when he was kind enough to give me the above-mentioned Italian review of *Mary Stuart,* which till then I had neither seen nor heard of. I shall like also to see what you say of me in *Harper*. I am truly obliged by your compliance with my request not to cite me—who have never yet gone in for autobiography—as a chronicler of myself. (Indeed I have never condescended to contradict even the most offensive and outrageous reports printed of me in the viler journals.) No truth-teller, I venture to believe, could print of me anything that was otherwise than "honourable," but it would certainly be less than "agreeable to myself" to appear as an autobiographer by proxy.

Have you seen Mr. Hall Caine's collection of sonnets past and present? It has had or is having a great and (I think) well-deserved success; but my sonnets on Carlyle's venomous *Reminiscences* have excited a most amusing and gratifying amount of wrath among the posthumous sycophants of that virulent old sophist.

The only time I ever saw Mr. Oscar Wilde was in a crush at our acquaintance, Lord Houghton's. I thought he seemed a harmless young nobody, and had no notion he was the sort of man to play the mountebank, as he seems to have been doing. A letter which he wrote to me lately about Walt Whitman was quite a modest, gentleman-like, reasonable affair without any flourish or affectation of any kind in matter or expression. It is really very odd. I should think you in America must be as tired of his name as we are in London of Mr. Barnum's and his Jumbo's.

Mr. Watts, with whom I now keep house, sends his kind regards to you; and I remain
Yours very sincerely,
A. C. SWINBURNE.

LETTER LVI

To Lord Houghton

*The Pines,
Putney Hill,
S.W.
June 6th,* 1882.

DEAR LORD HOUGHTON,
      I have been working harder than ever I worked yet on an article for the *Encyclopædia Britannica*—"Mary Queen of Scots." Having been persuaded to undertake it, I would of course spare no pains to ensure its accuracy and completeness—and I really think it is a good piece of narrative and study of character. I have simply, in the relation of events, set down facts admitted on all hands as indisputable, relegating every incident or detail that has ever been questioned to the apocryphal region of hypothesis or rumour, and then stated the question of character as it appears on this evidence alone.

Yesterday I despatched the last sheets of the last revise of my new volume. *If* the British Matron can get over two Cantos (the 2nd and 4th) of my *Tristram,* I expect the Mothers of England to rally round a book containing forty-five "songs of innocence"—lyrics on infancy and childhood. In token thereof I send you the list of contents.

Ever yours truly,
A. C. SWINBURNE.

LETTER LVII

To Edmund Gosse

Wednesday.
[June 7th, 1882.]

MY DEAR GOSSE,

On Friday evening at 8 I hope to see three or four friends here to a "reading" and supper. Will you come? I shall like to know what you—being an expert or a specialist in the matter, like myself—think of certain Sonnets [1] on the English Dramatists which I have lately written.

Ever yours sincerely,
A. C. SWINBURNE.

---

[1] These were the *Sonnets on English Dramatic Poets* (1590-1650), which occupy pp. 279-299 of the *Tristram of Lyonesse* volume, published in July, 1882.

LETTER LVIII

To A. H. Bullen

*The Pines,
Putney Hill,
S.W.
June 13th,* 1882.

Dear Sir,
I have just received your beautiful volume of Old Plays.[1] The *Nero* is an old acquaintance of mine, whom I am glad to see in handsomer attire than his old coat of 1624, especially as a fine copy of that quarto, which I had for many years, seems to have taken wing somehow out of my little collection.[2] Southey, in his *Doctor,* if I remember aright, includes it in a list of the anonymous works whose authors he would be especially glad to unearth.

There are two plays, unreprinted, and unincluded in your list, which must, I should think, be of some interest, even if not of any great value: the anonymous *Wars of Cyrus*,[3] 1594, unique, accord-

---

[1] *A Collection of Old English Plays.* Edited by A. H. Bullen. Privately printed, 1882.
[2] It was, however, found eventually; and, after Swinburne's death, was sold by Watts-Dunton to Mr. Wise.
[3] *The Warres of Cyrus, King of Persia, against Antiochus, King of Asyria, with the tragical End of Panthaea.*

ing to Lamb, whose extract from the Chorus has always excited my curiosity: and *Cynthia's Revenge*,[1] 1613, to which Ben Jonson prefixed commendatory verses. These, and B. Barnes's MS. *Battle of Evesham*, if procurable, would surely be very welcome to students.

Meantime, with all thanks for what you are already giving us,
    I remain,
      Yours very faithfully,
        A. C. SWINBURNE.

P.S.—I enclose a cheque for £1 1s.
There are two unreprinted historical Plays, not on your list, which I am anxious to see—Nabbes's *Hannibal and Scipio*, 1637; and *The Costlie Whore*,[2] 1633, which according to Mr. Halliwell-Phillips "has considerable merit." And, if only on account of his association with greater dramatists, I should have thought that Robert Daborne's two Plays, *A Christian turned Turk* and *The Poor Man's Comfort*,[3] must be worth reprinting.

You will excuse the intrusion of these suggestions from a fellow-lover of our old dramatists.

---

[1] The anonymous author of *Cynthia's Revenge* was a member of the Society of Lincoln's Inn, of whom nothing else is known.

[2] Both these plays were privately reprinted by Mr. Bullen, *Hannibal and Scipio* in 1887, and *The Costlie Whore* in 1885.

[3] Daborne's plays remain (in 1918) inaccessible.

P.P.S.—I re-open this letter to add a note on a small point of verbal criticism.

The phrase (p. 138) "Whatten a God might that be" is good Northumbrian to this day for "what manner" or "what sort of God—?" whence I guess the author of *The Maids Metamorphosis* to have been a fellow-countryman of mine.

LETTER LIX

To A. H. Bullen

The Pines,
Putney Hill,
S.W.
June 19th, 1882.

Dear Sir,

I must allow that your account of *Cynthia's Revenge* tallies accurately enough with my own impression, derived from a brief examination, or rather inspection, of it years ago; but even were it as tedious as *Cynthia's Revels* I would—were it reprinted—give it one reading for the sake of rare Ben, who possibly lent it a puff out of satisfaction at finding a play devoted to Cynthia even longer and duller,—if it be so—than his own. But I doubt if such an "if" be possible.

I think you are—as I told Dr. Grosart, when he

reprinted Barnes's Poems,[1] that I thought he was too hard on *The Devil's Charter*. There are dull parts and nauseous passages in it, but the scene between Cæsar Borgia and Catherine Sforza—from which Mr. Dyce thought that Shakespeare had taken a hint for stage business in *The Tempest*—is in my opinion decidedly good, spirited, and effective in a simple and straightforward way. And even if the *Battle of Evesham* were all but worthless as literature—were it (as it hardly, I think, can be) even as dull and feeble and empty as *The Life and Death of Jack Straw* [2]—yet, like that abortion of a bad Play, it must have considerable interest as giving an Elizabethan dramatist's view of an important crisis in the history of mediæval England. This historical and empirical interest would surely make it well worth preservation from the "dry-rot" to which you commend it.

I shall be glad to see Nabbes reprinted in full,[3] though I think (as far as I know him) he is a disappointing poet—promising (*e.g.* at the opening of *Tottenham Court*) more and better than he performs. But of course I should be delighted to find him better than I fear.

[1] The dramatic works of Barnabe Barnes remain unedited, but Dr. Grosart reprinted long scenes from *The Devil's Charter* (1607) in 1875.
[2] *Jack Straw's Life and Death* (1593) was entered at the Stationers' Company by John Dancer.
[3] This was done by Mr. Bullen, in two volumes, in 1887.

I am sincerely gratified to know that my studies on Ford and Chapman did for you something of what Lamb did for me when a boy at Eton. My own impression is that every English Play in existence down to 1640 must be worth reprinting on extrinsic if not on intrinsic grounds.

Yours very faithfully,
A. C. SWINBURNE.

LETTER LX

To Edmund Gosse

<i>The Pines,
Putney Hill,
S.W.
June 24th,</i> 1882.</div>

My dear Gosse,

I had hardly put down Watts's copy of your *Gray* when the copy you were kind enough to send me arrived. I thank you very sincerely for it, and congratulate you on a successful and delightful piece of work. It must have been a labour of love, and one which needed a love of labour for its accomplishment.

The book is unquestionably one of the very few jewels of a most singularly unequal series[1]—of which I should say that some volumes were about

---

[1] *English Men of Letters,* edited by John Morley.

as bad as possible, others—perhaps more—very fairly creditable, and two or three about as good as they could be. I need not say that yours belongs unmistakably to my third class. As to the *Odes,* we may as well agree to differ. About the Norse poems I agree with you as heartily as about the *Elegy.* Did I ever tell you from whose lips it was that I, when a little boy, first heard the unforgettable anecdote of Wolfe's tribute to that poem? Wordsworth's—who related it to my parents on the one occasion on which I was presented to him [1] a month or two before his death.

This *Gray,* with *Byron, Landor,* and *Spenser,* makes up, I think, the quadrilateral of thoroughly good books in the series. Perhaps I should add *Goldsmith* to the four.

Yours very sincerely,
A. C. SWINBURNE.

LETTER LXI

To Edmund Gosse

The Pines.
July 25th, 1882.

MY DEAR GOSSE,
  I cannot but send you one little word in assurance of my keenest and warmest sympathy

[1] In September, 1849.

with your late terrible anxiety,[1] and in congratulation on its removal. I could hardly (I think) feel more sympathy if I had ever myself passed through the ordeal of such a time. But I know parents can hardly be expected to believe that "a barren stock" (to borrow Queen Elizabeth's phrase) can be capable in imagination of entering into their emotions.

The hearing of the little thing's first words, uttered as they were in pain, must indeed have given you a sense of awe as well as of tenderness and terror.

To come down to the subject of poetry—I am particularly pleased by your preference for my Sonnets on the firm of Marlowe, Shakespeare, and Co. I think *Athens,* unquestionably, far away my best ode, though I hope to match it by one on the religions of the world, for which I have drawn up a sketch or summary of contents in prose outline to be filled in hereafter.

Yours very sincerely,
A. C. SWINBURNE.

[1] The dangerous illness of Mr. Gosse's infant son.

LETTER LXII

To Edmund Gosse

Wednesday.
[Postmark, August 3rd, 1882],
between 11 and 12 p.m.

My dear Gosse,
On returning home with my head full of your Massinger discoveries,[1] I remember that Gifford, after the appearance of his first edition, discovered a copy of *The Duke of Milan* corrected by the author—an undoubted autograph—exactly after the fashion of your quartos. This is an additional evidence in favour of the authenticity of the marginal notes in your copies.

Ever sincerely yours,
A. C. Swinburne.

---

[1] Mr. Gosse had acquired, as the gift of John Addington Symonds, a volume of first quartos of Massinger with numerous corrections and interpolations which seem to be in the handwriting of that poet. Swinburne had paid a visit to 29, Delamere Terrace, for the express purpose of examining this volume, which he did with the result indicated above.

LETTER LXIII

To Edmund Gosse

The Pines.
August 9th, 1882.

My dear Gosse,
    I have this minute found lying unbeknown inside Watts's copy of *The Unbeknown Eros*[1] two adorable photographs of two "friends havin' the pleasure of bein' beknown," addressed to me in your handwriting. Accept a thousand thanks, and transmit a thousand loves and kisses to the friends in question from
    Yours ever sincerely,
    A. C. Swinburne.

[1] Coventry Patmore and his *Unknown Eros* were the subjects of unceasing sarcasm from Swinburne. The "friends" immediately afterwards mentioned were Philip and Sylvia, Mr. Gosse's younger children.

LETTER LXIV

To John Churton Collins

*The Pines,
Putney Hill,
S.W.
September 21st,* 1882.

MY DEAR COLLINS,
I know nobody so likely as you to be able to verify the first four quotations of the five enclosed, which have been sent to me by the latest biographer of Lamb [1] with a request that I would, if possible, tell him whence they come. The fifth, of course, is from *Comus*. The fourth is so absolutely familiar to my ear that I am exasperated with vexation at being unable to bring my memory to book with any certainty as to the context. I feel all but confident it is Fletcher—but I have hunted in vain through two or three plays. I know it as well as "To be or not to be"—and it is most irritating to be perpetually baulked when I try to spot it.

"Talking of boots" you must remind me some day to show you the text of Hamlet's soliloquy as edited by Mr. Carew Hazlitt (MS. *penes me*) after the fashion of his text of *The Revenger's*

[1] Alfred Ainger (1837-1904).

Tragedy. I was reading your preface to Tourneur last evening, which reminded me of this valuable specimen of critical ability by the brief and moderate castigation therein administered in passing to that monstrous incarnation of duncery.

I believe I have never yet thanked you for a letter in acknowledgment of *Tristram* which gave me real pleasure. I do so now, and remain
Ever sincerely yours,
A. C. SWINBURNE.

Please return the slip of paper enclosed.

LETTER LXV

To John Churton Collins

The Pines,
September 29th [1882]

My dear Collins,

I felt a dark sense of error—such a sense as an unhappy sceptic may feel when first assailed by doubts as to the moral character of the Most High, as self-revealed to His servant Moses, and self-recorded in a volume which I will not mention by name—after I had sent off my last letter to your old address. But I could not find *your* last letter. I had put it away somewhere to keep, and that is the way to lose sight of anything—and I have now only to thank a beneficent Providence that you ever got mine at all. I am very sorry you are in the same irritating state of obliviousness or nescience with myself, especially if it worries and chafes you as it does me to hunt and catch and lose again the scent of a half-recognized quotation.

Purnell [1] dined here with us, the day before yesterday or so, to discuss certain sonnets. I want, now as always, to be of any service to him—and I hope he may make a success of his sonnet-book. I could not at once remember what was the last enterprise of the Bad Shepherd who makes his living out of dead sheep (Thackeray in *Fraser,* is it not?), so that your outbreak of righteous wrath rather bewildered me at first. "What" (thought I to myself) "can that luckless pastor have been doing with other men's flocks this time, to incur such indignation?" After all, the worst I personally know of him is that he is associated with Carlyle Copronymus—foul company no doubt, but the dung-eating old dog associated in his time with many of his (and his Shepherd's) betters, whose bread he ate and whose graves he defiled.

I have not seen Tennyson on Virgil.[2] It is a pity and a shame if it is not good, for on the one occasion when I (then an undergraduate) was favoured with any of the Laureate's conversation

---

[1] The dramatic critic, Thomas Purnell (1834-1889). Swinburne's letters to him were privately printed in 1910.
[2] *The Nineteenth Century,* September, 1882.

—very pleasant and hospitable it was—he expressed a special devotion for the Laureate of the first and hatefullest (to me) of all the emperors. Come soon (tho' I have not much to show you) and see—or hear—the very little I have been or am doing. Any day and hour will suit me (D.—I need not say V.), as I am not likely to stir again for some time.

I rather want something big to do, or at least attempt. The one great subject for historic tragedy which I have always thought of and recoiled from or put by—"The Life and Death of Cæsar Borgia"[1]—seems no less magnificent but more and more unmanageable, the more I think of it. The catastrophe—if his own reported words be accurate—is about the most *moral* thing I ever read of in history, and ought if dramatised accordingly, to conciliate the suffrages of the religious reading world: but what between triple incest, and the bisexual harem of the Vicar of Christ—points which could not be wholly ignored in a "chronicle history" of the Borgias—even I feel conscious of something like the sentiment called "funk" in face of the inevitable difficulties. Yet the triumph and fall (through his own triumphant wickedness) of

---

[1] All that Swinburne wrote of this projected tragedy was published in 1908, as *The Duke of Gandia*. The subject had attracted him at quite an early period, and fragmentary attempts made at Oxford in 1858 still survive.

the greatest warrior and statesman of his age might and should be an almost incomparable argument of tragic poetry.

Ever yours sincerely,
A. C. SWINBURNE.

LETTER LXVI

To A. H. BULLEN

October 8th, 1882.

DEAR SIR,
   I have very great pleasure in expressing my most sincere and grateful sense of the services you have already rendered to all serious students of English poetic literature in one of its highest, its most important, and its generally neglected branches. I know no books of their kind better edited than your *Old English Plays,* including the Works of John Day; and I trust these are but the first-fruits of a noble harvest yet to be gathered in. I am eagerly expecting the promised second volume of your collection.

I am sorry you gave such a poor account of the *Wars of Cyrus.* Of course I agree with your critical verdict as to the small value of the pre-Shakespearian anonymous dramas (with one or two notable exceptions)—but the poorest of them must surely have some accidental or empirical interest, even if no literary merit of its own.

Mr. Ainger, the biographer of Charles Lamb, has written to ask me if I can verify for him one or two quotations in the *Essays of Elia*. Two of these, familiar to my ear as any household word even of Shakespeare's, I find myself (to my great disgust and self-contempt) unable to trace.

> *One that's born and has his years come to him* [1]
> *In some green desert.*
>
> *Unworthy land to harbour such a sweetness,* [2]
> *A virtue wherein all the ennobling thoughts dwelt,*
> *Pure thoughts, brave thoughts, high thoughts, her sex's wonder!*

(I transcribe from memory, but I think, accurately.) Can you help us? It will very much oblige.

Yours sincerely,
A. C. SWINBURNE.

P.S.—Your letter of the 2nd has only to-day reached me in the country.

[1] This is quoted from Middleton's *Mayor of Quinborough* (1661), Act I., sc. 1; but Middleton's text reads "in a rough desart."

[2] This remains untraced, and there can be little doubt that it is Lamb's own.

LETTER LXVII

To A. H. Bullen

*Leigh House.
October 13th,* 1882.

Dear Sir,
Many thanks for the cutting from *Notes and Queries* concerning Lamb, which I read with interest and sympathy.

The quotation "Unworthy land," etc., is certainly, if I may for once speak positively on the negative side of a question, not Massinger's. That it does not come from any dramatist I think is the more probable assumption. It is the "green desert" that I really want to *spot;* for that, I feel certain, does.

The hideous and vilely edited six volumes of Moxon's *Lamb* contain I suspect all his articles now traceable, though perhaps the "Peter's Net" of the *London Magazine* may not have been thoroughly overhauled in search of strong squibs or "Jewels five words—or lines—long."

After all, is it not possible that "Unworthy land" is a specimen of some second unfinished or fragmentary *John Woodvil?* The other I thought was in *A King and no King,* but it is not.

I think I told you of my treasured Lamb MSS.

—the unpublished note on Wither and "most negative Nott."[1] I wonder what the dung-dropping mouth of Carlyle would have said to them!

Excuse a vile pen, and believe me,
Yours very sincerely,
A. C. SWINBURNE.

LETTER LXVIII

To Edmund Gosse

Hôtel de Lille et d'Albion,
Rue St. Honoré 223,
Paris.
November 22nd, 1882.

MY DEAR GOSSE,
I must not be late by one post longer than I can help in acknowledging your kindness, and thanking you cordially for the Memoir of Lodge,[2] which I look forward to reading with great interest and pleasure on my return to England to-morrow. Your note of the 18th announcing the gift has just reached me here, on the morning of the great event which has brought me

---

[1] See Swinburne's *Miscellanies*, 1886, pp. 157-200. This delightful volume, with Lamb's copious MS. annotations, is now in the possession of Mr. J. A. Spoor, of Chicago.

[2] Thomas Lodge (1558?-1625), whose *Works* Mr. Gosse had lately introduced, for the first time, for the Hunterian Club.

SWINBURNE'S LETTERS

to Paris—the resurrection of *Le Roi s'amuse*. This second night of the greatest play since Shakespeare is—as you probably know—the fiftieth anniversary of its first representation; a thing as unique and wonderful as the play itself.

Yours very sincerely,
A. C. SWINBURNE.

LETTER LXIX

To Madame Tola Dorian

Paris.
November 22, 1882.

MADAME,

Vous avez fait parler à mes vers [1] la langue du Maître aux pieds duquel je les ai mis; je vous en remercie du plus profond de mon cœur. Il manquait à mon ode des ailes pour franchir la mer: c'est grâce à vous qu'elle n'est plus insulaire.

ALGERNON CHARLES SWINBURNE.

---

[1] *The Statue of Victor Hugo,* translated into French verse by Madame Tola Dorian. This was the pseudonym adopted for her numerous writings by the Princess Mestchersky. She brought out in 1883 a French version of *The Cenci* of Shelley, which gained Swinburne's approval.

LETTER LXX

To John Churton Collins

*The Pines,
Putney Hill,
S.W.*
November 30th, 1882.

My dear Collins,
            I fear you will think me very dull if I confess that I do not see or believe in any recondite law or principle in Shakespeare's use of prose whenever he felt himself more at ease, for his purpose of the moment, in prose than in verse. Of course his range of command in the one province was almost as wonderful as in the other, and he had an unequalled capacity of adapting it to the requirements of the subject, from Hamlet's meditation on man to Falstaff's catechism on honour: but I at all events am unable to recognize any deeper or subtler line of demarcation traceable between its varieties of tone and style than might be required by the exigencies of the matter in hand.

There are two reasons against my going to see the Cantabrigian *Ajax* with you, though it is very friendly of you to think of it: I should find myself too deaf (as last week at the Théâtre Français) to hear a line of the text, however well delivered, and two oblivious (or, if you prefer it, too great a dunce) to follow it if I could. When the wives of Heads of Houses and married Fellows get up the *Lysistrata* (with a due selection of eligible undergraduates) on a public stage—then, if invited to that Attic spectacle, I will not (D.V.) be wanting.

I have just been making some few annotations and corrections in your admirable edition of Tourneur, which are at your service when (or if) the idiot public has the sense to require a re-issue of the book. I do think the neglect of that superb genius, when so adequately presented and introduced to the notice of readers, is the grossest instance of general stupidity and torpor in literary taste and English scholarship that ever I witnessed.

Always sincerely yours,
A. C. SWINBURNE.

LETTER LXXI

To Mrs. Ionides

*The Pines,
    Putney Hill,
      S.W.*
        Jan. 12th, 1883.

DEAR MRS. IONIDES,

Thank you a thousand times for your beautiful New Year's gift. I hardly know which of the two photographs is the more charming. An art-critic, aged eight, who was in my room when they arrived, observed that the doll was very bad, but admitted that the little girl was very good, which, as I did not fail to point out, might perhaps be considered a sufficiently satisfactory result to make up for the undeniable shortcomings of the doll.

If you will come and see me, I will show you the most successful photograph (on a somewhat larger scale than these) of a beautiful child [1] that ever I saw—the daughter of a Russian princess by birth and nihilist by profession—as perhaps I need not have added, for I flatter myself that when I mention any Russian as a personal friend it can scarcely be requisite to specify which party in the empire has the honour of that Russian's adherence.

With renewed thanks, and kind regards to Mr. Ionides as to yourself, believe me,

Yours very truly,
A. C. SWINBURNE.

[1] This was Dora Dorian, "child of two strong nations," to whom Swinburne addressed a rondeau.

LETTER LXXII

To A. H. Bullen

*The Pines,
Putney Hill,
S.W.*
March 12th, 1883.

MY DEAR SIR,
　　　　I am glad to have the mystery unriddled which had perplexed other students besides myself. Of course we all know that printers are like the prophet Habakkuk—according to Voltaire—capable of anything; and this an amusing instance of their perversity.

I agree with you in the attribution of *Captain Underwit*[1] to Shirley, and should place it, in point of interest and literary merit, very high on the list of his better works, though much impaired and deformed by that slovenly superfluity of underplot which is the damning plot of his school,—that is, of the disciples of Fletcher and Massinger who had lost (or rather had failed to learn) the skill of these masters in the combination or fusion of story with story. And "free" as some of this

---

[1] An anonymous comedy of about 1640, printed, for the first time, by Mr. Bullen, in his *Collection of Old English Plays*, Vol. II., in 1883.

play is, it is surely not grosser or looser than several of Shirley's best.

Barnavelt ought most assuredly to make his appearance in public, and I shall be very much gratified if my remarks can be of any service to you in the process of introduction. I read parts of the Play on Saturday to Mr. J. Churton Collins, the Editor of Cyril Tourneur and Lord Herbert of Cherbury, who was as much struck as yourself and your correspondents Messrs. Boyle[1] and Fleay,[2] by the likeness of style to Fletcher's here and Massinger's there,—till I also read him the first scene of the third Act of Brewer's *Country Girle,* where the resemblance to Massinger is even more striking than anywhere in *Barnavelt.* The metrical testers always overlook the very plain fact that Jonson, Fletcher, and Massinger had each his pupils and imitators of every degree of ability, from such men as Cartwright and Shirley, to such men as Davenant and Killigrew.

Yours sincerely,
A. C. SWINBURNE.

P.S.—I have just in time remembered one or two other things I had to say, with apology for their intrusion on your time and patience.

1. I wish, if possible to decipher, you would

---

[1] Mr. Robert Boyle, of St. Petersburg.
[2] The Rev. Frederick Gard Fleay.

give us the cancelled verses in the noble scene of Barnavelt's trial (p. 289).

2. I cannot but think it would be well worth while to print by subscription, though they may not be worth publication, most of the plays described in your very interesting Appendix. The historical interest of any—the dullest conceivable—historical play of that age must be surely sufficient to warrant and reward at least thus much trouble. The extract from *Edmund Ironside*,[1] though not excellent, is quite good enough to make me for one wish to read more of the play; and I should say the same of the sample given of *The Tragedy of Charlemagne*—or whatever other name would make it smell as sweet.

(Apropos of your note, p. 423) I am hardly "inclined to attribute *The Second Maiden's Tragedy* to Middleton." I only pointed out its likeness in some respects of style and composition to his tragic manner. I leave "attribution" to more self-confident experts. Also I at any rate should be glad to read *The Fatal Marriage, Richard II.* and Chapman's *Masque*—if his it be. But especially I want to see *The Two Noble Ladies* or *The Converted Conjurer,* as the first English version of Calderon's (and Shelley's) *Magico Pro-*

---

[1] *Edmund Ironside: The English King,* a MS. chronicle-play in the British Museum; it is still unedited, like several other pieces mentioned in this letter.

digioso, with the very names of hero and heroine in the original poem retained; though it must doubtless be a very poor and erratic version of the story. And surely *The Lancheinge of the May* must be doubly worth preservation—as a quasi-historical document, and as "a good jest for ever." The extract is delicious.—A.C.S.

LETTER LXXIII

To Edmund Gosse

*The Pines,
Putney Hill,
S.W.
March 13th,* 1883.

MY DEAR GOSSE,

Far be it from me to incur the judgment of Uzza—and of Mason! I must decline to touch the Ark of Gray's verse,[1] even for the pur-

---

[1] The beautiful *Stanzas to Mr. Richard Bentley,* written in 1752, exist in a single MS., and the corner of the last stanza was torn off when Mason found it. It reads:—

> *Enough for me, if to some feeling breast,
> My lines a secret sympathy
> And as their pleasing influence
> A sigh of soft reflection*

Mason, Mitford and others have volunteered endings to the three mutilated lines, but their additions are not convincing. As Swinburne refused to intervene, Mr. Gosse printed the verses in the fragmentary form given above.

pose of lending it a prop! Have you asked your friend Mr. Browning to perform this office? or has he too shrunk from the responsibility?

Your proposed test for the metrical testers is very fair, and I have written a long letter on the subject to Mr. Bullen in answer to a note from him explaining how Milton's line slipped into his text thro' carelessness in revision of proofs. But the question—"Who wrote *Barnavelt's Tragedy?*"—remains debatable on wider grounds of argument, and very interesting. When are you going to make public your valuable discovery of apparently autographic corrections in your copies of Massinger's plays? I kiss the hands and feet of the young lady [1] whose photograph—constantly referred to and gazed on with yearning eyes—ever more deeply enthralls my heart, and remain.

    Yours very sincerely,
      A. C. SWINBURNE.

[1] Sylvia Laura Gosse.

LETTER LXXIV

To Edmund Gosse

> The Pines,
> Putney Hill,
> S.W.
> *March* 28th, 1883.

My dear Gosse,

Many thanks for your interesting article on Crashaw. I wrote one myself at the age of nineteen, but it never saw the light, and long since probably fed the fire. Of course you are right in supposing that my *Song in Season* was suggested or instigated by his shorter attempt in the same metre, which always greatly took my fancy; as did also *Love's Horoscope*—one of the most nearly blameless among his poems, which I am glad to find a favourite of yours as well as of my own. I am too busy with verse-making just now to revert to the criticism of *Barnavelt*,[1] which I may take up again in *The Athenæum* when I have completed a little book of Songs,[2] now nearly ready for publi-

---

[1] The anonymous Tragedy of *Sir John van Olden Barnavelt* was for the first time printed by Mr. A. H. Bullen, in 1883, in Vol. II. of his *Collection of Old English Plays*. Mr. Bullen attributed it to Massinger. Swinburne detected in it a line of Milton, and there ensued some controversy in *The Athenæum*.

[2] *A Century of Roundels*, 1883.

cation, which till then occupies me more pleasantly than prose. (Excuse—as Landor would not have done—two "witches" in a sentence.)

Ever sincerely yours,
A. C. SWINBURNE.

LETTER LXXV

TO EDMUND GOSSE

*The Pines,
Putney Hill,
S.W.
September 8th, 1883.*

MY DEAR GOSSE,

I return, as you desire, the letter and enclosure which I have just received. I am of course very sorry to hear of Mr. Stedman's distress, and touched by his considerate recollection of the fact that I had provisionally accepted his invitation to become a guest under his roof if ever I went to New York. I agree with you that the tone of his letter is very manful and creditable. Watts joins me in expressing his deep sympathy with Mr. Stedman.[1] He asks me at the same time

---

[1] The reference is to Edmund Clarence Stedman (1833-1908), the banker-poet of New York, who had repeatedly urged Swinburne to come to America and to be his guest. Swinburne, though loath to travel, had not positively refused. But in August, 1883, the firm of E. C. Stedman & Co. sus-

to tell you that a letter from you to him written some weeks since, reaching here during his absence in Oxfordshire, got unfortunately mislaid, and has but just come to hand. He will answer it.

Ever sincerely yours,
A. C. SWINBURNE.

pended payment on the Stock Exchange, in consequence of the transactions of a younger partner. The business of the house had not been large, but it had been considered safe and prosperous. Sympathy was widely felt for the banker-poet, who was thus reduced almost to indigence by speculations which he had not authorised. In a very pathetic letter of August 27th, 1883, to Mr. Gosse, Stedman described the conditions in which he had lost his little fortune, and concluded as follows:—

"You can do me a favour by incidentally telling my friends of the situation. One thing in particular: Mr. Swinburne has talked of visiting America ere long, and had written me that he should make my house his home in New York. It would greatly distress me to be misunderstood by you, or by him. Should you see him, you might mention these things, mortifying as they are. Not that I shall not be delighted to welcome my friends as heretofore; but I should be embarrassed to have my hospitalities be thought churlish."

LETTER LXXVI

To Edmund Gosse

*The Pines,
Putney Hill,
S.W.
October 24th, 1883.*

MY DEAR GOSSE,
    I must write to thank you for your delightful book [1] even before I cut the leaves open. It will be equally a pleasure to make and to renew acquaintance with those of its contents which I have read and those which I have not. I am much gratified by your friendly mention of me in the preface—though I do not remember when or where I have ventured on "censure" of your excellent work in any part. I cannot say which is the best essay, but I think it no small compliment to say that one which still seems to me the most brilliantly successful on glancing thro' the leaves is that which is incomparably the highest in subject. After all the homage which has been paid to Webster, it is a great thing to have written so freshly, and thrown such bright new light, on the work of so great a poet.
    Remember me kindly to Mrs. Gosse, and—if

---

[1] *Seventeenth Century Studies*, 1883.

remembrance be possible—to the children. I often think of the adorable sight I had once of Miss or Mistress Sylvia (the pre-Restoration title chimes most fitly with the sweet Elizabethan name) attempting the untimely feat of getting out (unassisted) on the balcony with perpetually frustrated perseverance and renascent hope—I never saw anything (or anybody) more memorably pretty.

Ever sincerely yours,
A. C. SWINBURNE.

LETTER LXXVII

To Edmund Gosse

The Pines,
Putney Hill,
S.W.
February 4th, 1884.

My dear Gosse,

Of course I shall be most happy to sign the memorial.[1] I feel so strongly the weight of Philip Marston's claim, by right of genius as well as of adversity, that any use which could be made of my name, or any means by which I could be

---

[1] This was an appeal to Gladstone, as First Lord of the Treasury, to award a pension from the Civil List to the blind poet, Philip Burke Marston. The application was refused, and the disappointment told upon the health of Marston, which from this time forth rapidly declined.

of service to him or testify to my deep regard for the man and my cordial appreciation of the writer, would give me very great pleasure.

Ever sincerely yours,
A. C. SWINBURNE.

LETTER LXXVIII

To A. H. BULLEN

*The Pines,
Putney Hill,
S.W.
Feb.* 13, 1883 [*sic for* 1884].

MY DEAR SIR,

I really want words to thank you for the precious volume [1] I have this morning received. It is a great delight to see *Doctor Dodipoll* (as one might say) in the flesh. *Sir G[iles] G[oose-cap]* I glanced at in the Bodleian last year, but had not time to examine him. The two others must in any case be welcome as valuable curiosities at the very least.

But above all other unreprinted treasures I want, in the name and interest of English poetry, to see *The Costly Whore* restored to the light, and made accessible, without having recourse to the Douce collection. For sustained interest and artis-

[1] *A Collection of Old English Plays.* Edited by A. H. Bullen. Vol. III. Privately printed, 1884.

tic simplicity in development of story, for majestic beauty and dignity of poetic style, it seems to me unsurpassed by any work of Massinger's, and unequalled by the work of any other known playwright after the death of Fletcher.

On re-reading your letter of last March, I am inclined to think you have made a stronger case out for Massinger's partial authorship of *Barnavelt*[1] than I thought at first. It seems to me (in part) now rather a work of that master than merely a work of his school.

You have not sent anything with this volume to remind me what I have to remit to you, and in the multiplicity of other matters pressing upon me just now, I am not sure of anything except that the amount was very slight in return for so much pleasure.

I wish you could unearth B. Barnes's *Battle of Evesham,* if only on historic grounds. Any historical play of that date must be precious, even on a subject of less interest and importance.

Excuse my troubling you yet again with the obtrusion of my own wishes and solicitudes,

    And believe me,
        Yours sincerely,
           A. C. SWINBURNE.

[1] *Sir John Van Olden Barnavelt,* a play first printed by Mr. Bullen, in 1883, and attributed by him to Fletcher and Massinger.

LETTER LXXIX

To Paul Hamilton Hayne [1]

*The Pines,
Putney Hill,
S.W.
July 4th,* 1884.

My dear Mr. Hayne,
 I must not let a day pass without acknowledging the receipt of your letter and the poem enclosed in it.

The verses give a charming idea of the song they so lovingly describe. I am sorry to hear you speak of your feeble health and the improbability of your ever visiting England. Of course I shall be delighted to receive a copy of your "complete edition." If you should send it and receive no acknowledgment by return of post, please understand that I must at the time have been away from home; which I usually leave for some time during the summer and autumn.

I do know a little of Mr. Burroughs' writings, and hope some day to know more. He seems to hold among your writers much the same place that Mr. Richard Jefferies (author of *The Gamekeeper at Home, The Amateur Poacher,* etc., etc.,) holds

[1] Paul Hamilton Hayne (1830-86), the American poet.

among ours,—that of an eloquent and subtle, studious and humorous worshipper of nature.

As to Byron I have said my last word, with full and final deliberation. I think Poe, like Shelley, one of the very worst critics of poetry that ever existed; which does not diminish one whit my admiration for his exquisite genius. You will remember that he thought poor old Mr. Horne, lately deceased, one of the greatest poets of the century. The poem you mention is not even verse. How do you, or how did Poe, or how, for that matter, did Byron, propose to scan this line?—

In the wide waste there still is a tree.

That is not so much bad metre or harsh metre as no metre at all. I defy anybody to read or sing that line, as it stands, so as to make verse, even bad verse, of it; and for this reason—that it is very bad prose, lumbering, limping, and dissonant. Poe himself could not have written such a line, nor, I am convinced, could you.

Byron has written hundreds upon thousands as bad. And I hope he is almost the only man who ever did.

So much for the singer. As for the thinker I cannot imagine what your imagination can persuade you to see in *Manfred* that can be called imaginative. As dramatic figures, Manfred and Astarte are surely inferior to Punch and Judy;

and for those poorest of poor devils in the "Hall of Arimanes," if they could not put a little more spirit into their deviltry they would be hooted and hissed off the stage of any penny theatre in the world. There is not one scene, there is not one conception, in all the three acts of ranting rhetoric and guidebook descriptions, actually realized and vivified for a single second. I will find something better in the obscurest of the Elizabethans commemorated in those sonnets which I am delighted to hear that you like so well,—poets of whom Byron always spoke with the blatant insolence of stupid and vulgar ignorance.

Thanks for your suggestion about my poems on childhood. I should like very well to see them brought together in a book, but I leave all that sort of thing entirely to my publishers. If they thought it would pay I suppose they would suggest it. When my forthcoming volume is out,[1] I shall have published fifty poems on a single child[2] (whom I have just seen playing at see-saw in the broiling sun), all written between his sixth and his tenth birthdays.

Ever sincerely yours,
A. C. SWINBURNE.

[1] *A Midsummer Holiday and Other Poems.*
[2] Edward Mason, Watts-Dunton's nephew.

LETTER LXXX

To Lord Morley

The Pines,
Putney Hill, S.W.
July 12th, '84.

MY DEAR MORLEY,
I have just that vague recollection of the passage you want, which is worse than none at all. I fancy it must be in some one of Byron's wretched plays, for it is not (as far as I have had time to look) where I guessed it might be—in the *Prophecy of Dante*.

Ever yours,
A. C. SWINBURNE.

LETTER LXXXI

To A. H. Bullen

The Pines,
Putney Hill,
S.W.
August 8th, 1884.

MY DEAR SIR,
Of course you are most welcome to my old carol;[1] I wish it were better worth the honour

---

[1] *A Christmas Carol* (suggested by a drawing by D. G. Rossetti):

you intend it. But have you secured one which on a moderate computation is worth 1,000,000,000 of mine—W. Morris's published with music, I forget how many years since?[2] That one has always seemed to me the third—or rather one of the co-equal three finest (as far as I know) in the language—the two others being, *As Joseph was a-walking,* which everybody knows, and *I syng of a Mayden* (No. 25 in Wright's *Songs and Carols,* printed in 1856 for the Warton Club, I think; a society which only produced three other pamphlets, and then I believe gave up the ghost). I need not add that I never met anybody who knew this Carol, but everybody to whom I ever showed it agrees with me that it is one of the sweetest things in English verse. I picked up the pamphlet by accident years ago.

I wrote to you last year, after a visit to Oxford,

>   *Three damsels in the queen's chamber,*
>   *The queen's mouth was most fair; etc.*

printed in *Poems and Ballads,* First Series, 1866, pp. 251-254.
[2] Morris's *Carol* [*Masters, in this Hall,*] originally appeared in Sedding's *Ancient Christmas Carols,* 1860. It commences:

>   *To Bethlem did they go, the shepherds three;*
>   *To Bethlem did they go to see whe'r it were so or no,*
>   *Whether Christ were born or no*
>   *To set men free.*

Both *Carols* were reprinted in Bullen's *A Christmas Garland: Carols and Poems from the Fifteenth Century to the Present Time,* 1885, [actually issued in December, 1884].

a letter of some length, entreating you if possible to give us re-issues of two old plays (never yet reprinted), which I had been reading in the Bodleian; but as I never received an answer to my petition I supposed my letter might have miscarried. It was written, if I remember, on reception of your third (I hope and trust not your last) volume of *Old Plays*.

I am overwhelmed with shame at not having remembered that Lamb's quotation was from Middleton, a favourite poet of my own ever since my schooldays. I ought to have known that any verse so like Fletcher's must, if not his, be Middleton's.

Yours very sincerely,
A. C. SWINBURNE.

LETTER LXXXII

To A. H. BULLEN

The Pines,
Putney Hill,
S.W.
August 10th, 1884.

MY DEAR SIR,

I am much gratified by your proposal to dedicate your intended edition of Middleton to me, and I thank you sincerely for the compliment.

I could wish you were about to give us Rowley and Davenport, before giving a reprint of Shirley, at all events. I read *A new trick to cheat the Devil* last year at Oxford with very great interest. Davenport's two other Plays I had long possessed, and knew well. He seems to me, with allowance for all occasional faults of taste and weaknesses of style, a distinct and attractive figure among his contemporaries, and well deserving of revival.

I shall be very glad to see *The Costly Whore* made accessible; it is a very fine Play. Do you not think the very early date and the curious style of *The Wars of Cyrus* sufficient reasons for reprinting a Play not quite devoid of merit in its crude fashion, and absolutely inaccessible?

The Carol by Mr. Morris to which I referred in my reply to your last note appeared, I think, some years ago, with music, in a very small collection edited by a Mr. Sedding—I believe I spell the name right—but I have not got the book, or rather the pamphlet. It has never been reprinted that I know of. It is very different in style from the *Outlanders,* but quite as fine, and more (perhaps) of a genuine Carol.

Believe me, yours very sincerely,
A. C. SWINBURNE.

LETTER LXXXIII

TO FRANK D. THOMAS

September 21st, 1884.

MY DEAR SIR,
 I am sincerely gratified by your proposal to utilize my verses. They are heartily at your service, and so are the two or three companion poems which I am now about to publish on the same subject—*The Twilight of the Lords, A Word for the Country,* etc. All or any of these are entirely at your disposal, should the League[1] do me the honour to think they might be of use to a cause which I have not the less sincerely at heart that I think it better to serve as a private soldier than as a nominal officer in a body whose meetings and councils I should be unable to attend.
 Yours very sincerely,
 A. C. SWINBURNE.

[1] The Primrose League.

LETTER LXXXIV

To A. H. Bullen

*The Pines,
Putney Hill,
S.W.
January 14th,* 1885.

My dear Sir,
Many thanks for the very welcome gift of your beautiful and valuable edition of Marlowe.[1] I have placed it on my shelves side by side with the three volumes of Dyce's edition which I had in my bookcase at Eton thirty years ago and more.

It has given me great interest and satisfaction to examine the way in which you have discharged your glorious task of service to so glorious a memory; and I cannot better show the sincerity of my gratitude than by the frank avowal of as sincere a regret that you should have thought it worth while to reprint Horne's *Death of Marlowe*[2] in such company as Marlowe's own—no real kindness to the poor old man's memory, for whom I had a regard undestroyed though not unqualified

---

[1] In three volumes, 1885. Dyce's edition appeared in 1850.
[2] Richard Henry Hengist Horne (1803-84), the poet of *Orion,* published his little tragedy, *The Death of Marlowe,* in 1837.

by the fact that he certainly was, as a correspondent, what Carlyle used to call "an afflictive phenomenon." Even if I did not differ *toto cælo* from your estimate of its merit, I should no less feel bound to protest against the introduction of his play into an appendix which might have been made more valuable by a reprint such as you would have given (for the first time) of the hitherto worse than inedited *Lust's Dominion*[1]—which, though of course spurious (at least as it now stands) in the main, has things in it well worthy of Marlowe, and so much in his style that they might reasonably be taken for parts of an unfinished or remodelled Play originally (if but partially) from his hand. The impossibility of his authorship applies only to certain passages which we know he could not have written, and which may well have been added to his MS. by Dekker, Haughton, or Day.

I wish also (though this is no great matter) that you had given the Puritan scoundrel's articles of impeachment in full, if they were to be given at all, as Ritson did before you. The whole value or interest of the document depends on its being given in full; and, offensive and preposterous as are the cancelled articles, they help to show that

[1] *Lust's Dominion: or, The Lascivious Queen,* a tragedy published in 12mo in 1657, and attributed to Marlowe. It was adapted for the stage in 1671, as *Abdelazar,* by Aphra Behn.

the whole thing was either a bad joke or an impudent calumny. And, if any of the rubbish was to be reprinted, I do not see why any should be suppressed in a limited edition. It is not as if you were bringing out a school or college edition *in usum juventutis academicae.*

I wish your next service were to be rendered to Dekker.[1] It is really a discredit to his country that there should be no decent edition of a dramatist who (as Lamb said) "had poetry enough for anything." Middleton, having been once already well edited,[2] might wait—being certainly, to say the very least, not superior to Dekker as a poet; and Shirley, as far as I am concerned, might wait for ever. What we do imperatively want is an edition of Marston, Dekker, Heywood, and (I should say) Davenport,[3] fit to rank with Dyce's and Gifford's.

I am happy to see that you have not adopted the heterography (for orthography it is not) of the old quartos in the case of Marlowe. (Have you seen my *Encyclopædia Britannica* article on him? I fancy you may not have come across it, judging from your prefatory notice.)

[1] Dekker's Plays had been collected, in four volumes, by Herne Shepherd in 1873, but without any editorial care.
[2] By Dyce, in 1840. Mr. Bullen was at that moment preparing an excellent edition, which was completed in 1886.
[3] The *Works* of Robert Davenport were collected by Mr. Bullen in 1890.

You promised us (if I remember) a reprint of *Arden of Feversham,* and *Two Tragedies in One,* which I much want to see. And it is a pity that *The Costly Whore,* a really noble and interesting poem, should remain inaccessible because of a word in the title which—as Archbishop Trench justly observed, in a public lecture—is no more indecent really than the word "hireling," and means nothing more. But all these three points I believe I have pressed on you before.

I am glad to see by the notices of your book of Carols—not having seen the book—that you have secured for the collection that exquisite and incomparable Christmas song of Morris's which I believe I was the first to tell you of.

Yours very faithfully,
A. C. SWINBURNE.

I hardly agree with you about *Titus Andronicus.* The third and fourth scenes of the fourth act have always seemed to me hardly unworthy of the (very) young Shakespeare, and not very like any one else—unless, perhaps, Kid; certainly not Marlowe. And in the rest of the Play there are only here and there lines—never (or hardly ever) a Scene—good enough for *our* poet.

LETTER LXXXV

TO A. H. BULLEN

The Pines,
Putney Hill,
S.W.
January 19th, 1885.

MY DEAR SIR,
I have again to thank you for a beautiful and delightful book. No more welcome present than this and your Christmas Garland could have reached me at this still seasonable time of year. I only wish my undergraduate imitation of an old Carol were worthier of a place so near my friend Mr. Morris's perfect and incomparable examples; but no one can come within a thousand miles of him in any such field of work.

But I really want words to express my delight at the prospect of the forthcoming volume of your Old Plays. You are, it seems to me, quite right to keep *Arden*[1] for a separate reprint, on the ground you mention, and indeed on other grounds. I have lately seen for the first time the recast[2] of that wonderful play by Lillo for an

---
[1] *Arden of Feversham*, 1592, had been edited at Elberfeld, by Delius, in 1854; and was in 1887 reprinted by Mr. Bullen.
[2] George Lillo's *Arden of Feversham* was the latest of the plays of that dramatist, and was left unfinished at his death in 1739. It was acted at Drury Lane, but not printed until 1762. It was finished by John Hoadely.

eighteenth century audience—on which, according to Campbell, it produced on one occasion an almost Æschylean effect of terror, resulting in an inevitable interruption and suspension of the piece. As it is simply the old Play with all the poetry and half the passion squeezed out, I should more than ever like to see what would be the effect in our own day of a revival of the genuine text on the stage. I wish I had thought of proposing it to Irving one night which he spent at my chambers in London after the *Hamlet* of the evening was over, when we discussed my view and his rendering of the part till five o'clock in the morning.

I would not be thought to depreciate Shirley. I admire *The Traitor* and *The Lady of Pleasure* very cordially, and some others not very much less. But he seems to me colourless, formless, spiritless—or "wersh"[1] as we say in Northumberland—if compared with his predecessors; and while any of these remain unreprinted I grudge him the tribute of your valuable time and toil, and the honours of a second re-impression.

I dare say you are right about the authorship of *Lust's Dominion*. I took its identity with *The Spanish Moor's Tragedy* on trust from Dyce and

---

[1] The usual form of this Northumbrian word is "wairsh." It means sickly, faint, insipid. A great many variants are given in Wright's *English Dialect Dictionary* (Vol. VI., 1905).

Collier. But I think it deserves a decently careful edition.

Believe me, with renewed thanks,
>Yours very sincerely,
>>A. C. SWINBURNE.

LETTER LXXXVI

TO EDMUND GOSSE

*The Pines,
Putney Hill,
S.W.
February* 21*st,* 1885.

MY DEAR GOSSE,
You will wonder at not having got an answer from me to your very interesting letter of the 16th before now: the fact is that I have only this moment caught sight of it. I suppose it must have been laid on my table five days ago and then submerged—before I saw it—under other and less interesting papers. I am so deeply immersed in work just now that I have little time for correspondence—which must be my apology for a short as well as a tardy reply. I remember very well your admirable analysis of the play in question,[1] and wholly concur in your conclusion

---

[1] The tragi-comedy called *A Cure for a Cuckold*, attributed to Webster and Rowley.

as to the parts respectively assignable to Webster and Rowley.

Have you noticed the identity of motive between Webster's part of this play and the story of Montrose, Cleremont and Leonora in Massinger's *Parliament of Love?* I cannot but think that the two poets must have gone to a common source for the leading idea of their plots. Massinger's treatment of it is, I think, in his best manner—full of noble grace and dignity.

I am glad to hear of you home again, and to receive so agreeable an account of Whitman.[1] I retain a very cordial admiration for not a little of his earlier work; but the habit of vague and flatulent verbiage seems to me to have grown upon him instead of decreasing; and I must say it is long since I have read anything of his which seemed to me worthy of the nobler passages of his *Drum-Taps* and the earliest *Leaves of Grass*. However, you need not tell him so; but give him my cordial regards if ever you write to him.

With kindest remembrances to Mrs. Gosse and

---

[1] Mr. Gosse saw Walt Whitman in his house at Camden, New Jersey, in December, 1884. Whitman had asked about Swinburne, and had made several shrewd and on the whole amiable animadversions, of which Mr. Gosse had given a friendly report to the English Poet. The atmosphere, however, which now surrounded Swinburne was fatal to any continuance of his cordial appreciation of Whitman.

the little people—if they remember the existence of their humble but devoted servant—I remain,
Ever yours sincerely,
A. C. SWINBURNE.

LETTER LXXXVII[1]

To Edmund Gosse

*The Pines,
Putney Hill,
S.W.*
[*March 20th*, 1885.]

My dear Gosse,
Many thanks for a very pretty little book which I have just read through with pleasure. My only criticism shall be that the type is too small for the eyes of such readers as it seemingly appeals to. Nursery books ought to be printed with the types of a Baskerville or a Bodoni.
Ever yours truly,
A. C. SWINBURNE.

---

[1] This note would be too slight to merit publication, were it not that the "pretty little book" in question was R. L. Stevenson's *Child's Garden of Verses*. Of this author Mr. Gosse was, on many occasions, unable to extract a word of praise from Swinburne. Nor would he blame the friend of a friend; so that, whenever the name of Stevenson was brought up, Swinburne preserved an obstinate silence.

LETTER LXXXVIII

To A. H. Bullen

*The Pines,
Putney Hill,
S.W.
June 10th, 1885.*

My dear Sir,
I received the first four volumes of your most beautiful edition of *Middleton* last evening. I am very sincerely gratified by the high honour you have done me in dedicating them to me, whose best or only claim to that honour is his early regard for the poet—every line of whose works I had read (in Dyce's now eclipsed and superannuated edition) a year before I went to Oxford. It is a delight to look at such a book as this, and a source of pride to be in any way associated with it.

I am busier just now than I ever was before but once: for it is the second occasion in my life that I have ever undertaken to produce a piece of literary work by a given date. The first was when I undertook the Life of Mary Queen of Scots for the *Encyclopædia Britannica,* at very short notice, and I hope I may never have to undertake a third enterprise of writing against time.

SWINBURNE'S LETTERS

With most cordial thanks, and in eager expectation of the fourth volume of *Old Plays,*
I remain,
Yours sincerely,
A. C. SWINBURNE.

I must make time to congratulate you on the exquisite beauty of the masterly engravings in the first and the fourth volumes of *Middleton.*

LETTER LXXXIX

To Miss Alice Bird

*The Pines,
Putney Hill,
S.W.
June 20th,* '85.

DEAR MISS BIRD,
We shall both be delighted to come—that goes without saying. In the course of the evening Watts will have to go to the Academy swarry—Sir F. Leighton having sent each of us a card of invitation—but I think I shall excuse myself, as the swarry does not, I understand, consist of a boiled leg of mutton and trimmings, but will require a deal of standing or walking about, and an accident to my right foot has tied me fast to the house for more than a fortnight, but I am no longer such a cripple (happily) as to be unable

to accept your invitation. I wish you could be persuaded to visit us again—stay rather longer—and bring the Doctor; that his education in Natural History (of the age of Caxton) might be begun and your own completed.

Excuse bad ink and writing, and believe me,
Ever sincerely yours,
A. C. SWINBURNE.

LETTER XC

TO A. H. BULLEN

The Pines,
Putney Hill,
S.W.
July 10-24, 1885.

MY DEAR SIR,
The ill-will—to use no stronger word—of your *Pall-Mall* reviewer is too obvious to need unmasking; but, indeed, I have not yet seen a decent review of your *Middleton*. To do justice to it would need something of your own devotion, and your own knowledge of the subject—qualities which I presume you do not (any more than I should) expect to find in the average reviewer, be he who he may.

I am only too glad to accept your view of Fontinelle's character, considering the exquisite poetry put into his mouth—poetry worthy of the young Shakespeare.

I very much regret to hear that your publisher, as you say, "has arranged that Shirley should follow Middleton." On all accounts Shirley should come last—not that I would ignore or depreciate his merits, such as they are—but I can hardly express my disappointment and regret at the news that you are thinking of bestowing your precious time, labour, learning, and devotion on work which any honest hack might do, with Gifford's and Dyce's work before him. Shirley can surely wait for his turn, the last in date as the last in importance. And people will not read his voluminous and voluble improvisations—people, I mean, who would, if they were given a chance, read and profit by reading the works of his elders and betters. Dekker, Marston, Chapman, and Heywood are still inedited. Davenport, a poet at least the equal of Shirley, is not even reprinted. Here is a copious and a most fruitful field for your energy and scholarship.

Fresh editions of Beaumont and Fletcher, Massinger, Ford, are comparative superfluities—*articles de luxe*. I have been thirsting all my life for good editions of the poets I have mentioned, and it is most disheartening to find that we cannot expect from you this great service to English literature until an enterprise of so questionable and so hazardous a nature as this of your publisher has been carried through. Unless he is prepared to sink more money in it than he can well expect to see again, I should greatly fear that the result would simply be to disgust him with the very notion of publishing new editions of old dramatists. My own publishers were thinking of a similar scheme not many years ago, and I urgently dissuaded them from the project of reprinting Shirley. No doubt they would not have had nearly so competent an editor as yourself to give the enterprise even a chance of success: but, I must repeat, the time of such an editor might and should at present be far better employed.

With regard to your distaste for Marston's satires, I would suggest that it might be feasible to edit his dramatic works separately—as Dekker's, I should say, beyond all question ought to be. Dr. Grosart has printed a beautiful private edition of Marston's un-dramatic works, and is now bringing out Dekker's in a similar form: but after all it is the dramatic poet, in either case, whose claim to immortality is really serious and unquestionable; and it is this claim which you ought to have honour of establishing and making manifest. For myself, speaking as a lifetime student of this branch of English literature, I can sincerely say I would rather have an edition of Dekker's plays apart from his pamphlets, and would just as soon have an edition of Marston's plays apart from his satires. But such editions of these two Dramatists as you are now giving us of Middleton would be, in my poor opinion, the most valuable gifts of the kind that could be given to students of literature and lovers of poetry.

Then, I think, Robert Davenport should come next, and then Heywood. And before a new edition of Beaumont and Fletcher (or any poet who has had the good fortune to be edited by Dyce) is even thought of, a supplementary volume to the current editions of Ben Jonson ought surely to be undertaken. No service would be more acceptable to your fellow-students than the issue of such a volume, containing all the various readings of the quartos preceding the first folio of 1616—giving, of course, the full original text of *Every Man in his Humour*. This, by itself, would be a service which would ensure you the sincerest gratitude of all students—mine most especially. The last edition reprints the first act alone—a Vandal's version of the torture of Tantalus! This volume ought also to contain the full text of the interlude for the christening of Lord Newcastle's son, garbled by Gifford and Colonel Cunningham (Vol. IX. p. 327, ed. 1875), and perhaps the cancelled passages in the conversation with Drummond. It is really too absurd a pretence for his editors to play the Bowdler with Ben Jonson, of all men. But, anyhow, the varying versions, cancels, and corrections of his plays ought to be given, that justice may be done to so great and conscientious an artist: and this would be a work worthier of your ability and energy than the re-editing of Shirley.

Yours most sincerely,
A. C. SWINBURNE.

P.S.—You must forgive the delay of this letter —repeatedly interrupted, resumed, and interrupted again. The first critic living of English (and other) literature has just been expressing to me in very warm terms his admiration of your work as an editor, and his indignation (not to say disgust) at the systematic injustice and apparent envy or malevolence with which it has been received by the Press.

LETTER XCI

To A. H. BULLEN

The Pines,
Putney Hill,
S.W.
November 24th, 1885.

DEAR SIR,
  I snatch an hour from the revision of proofs and the transcription of extracts—the two

most grinding forms of toil I know—to apologize, in the first place, for the long and inexcusable delay in sending the small cheque now enclosed. Your later volumes came without any invoice, and I really did not know how much, in the way of money, I might not owe you. In a higher sense I did not know that I was indebted to you beyond all possible chance of repayment.

In writing on Middleton, as you will see (not next month, but the month after), I have expressed my sense of the inestimable value of your services to English literature and scholarship as fully as I could venture to do in face of the dedication with which you have honoured me. Perhaps I may be able to add a note on your elucidation of *A Game at Chess*. With all its difficulties, the really wonderful genius and variety of intelligence which animate every scene of that play make it still more delightful reading to me; and I look forward eagerly to the additional interest and pleasure which your illustrations of the text will give me.

I hardly know how to thank you in proper terms for the generosity of your promised gifts, as well as the Selections from Drayton, which I have not yet received, but shall value very highly. I have never gone as deep as I have often meant to go in study of that voluble and voluminous poet; but as to his great sonnet I can only say that to me it seems perfect as well as great. I cannot see any falling off in it. The change of note towards the end strikes me as perhaps the finest touch of music and feeling in any sonnet ever written. Its abruptness is so natural, the sudden relapse or return of passion on itself is so wonderfully true and pathetic, that I can remember nothing of the sort quite worthy to be set beside it. I wish any sonnet of mine was worth half or less than half of that one; but I am very sincerely and cordially gratified by what you say of some among my later attempts in that line.

Believe me,
Yours most truly,
A. C. SWINBURNE

P.S.—I read Yarrington's (*sic*) play [1] with great interest; it has real pathos, and genuine realistic power. But it has more in common with *A Warning for Fair Women* than with *Arden of Feversham*. The incomparable style of the latter—its superb combination of poetic dignity with perfect truthfulness—its passion, imagination, and instructive rectitude of dramatic touch—are qualities of which I see no comparable trace in the two others.

---

[1] *Two Lamentable Tragedies* (1601); a double murder-play by Robert Yarington, which Mr. Bullen had reprinted in Vol. IV. of his *Old English Plays*, 1885.

LETTER XCII

To A. H. Bullen

*The Pines,
Putney Hill,
S.W.*
January 1st, 1886.

Dear Sir,
I send you the first copy I receive of *The Nineteenth Century* for this month. If I have said less than I otherwise might have said in direct praise of your personal work as Editor, it is (of course) that I felt my freedom of speech somewhat hampered by consideration of the compliment paid to me in the dedication of the book. But I hope you will think that adequate or at least tolerable justice has been done to the poet.

I am eager to see your commentary on that masterpiece of patriotic and poetic ingenuity, *A Game at Chess.* How highly I rate that play on re-perusal you will see by my article.

I must thank you again for your beautiful *Drayton;* I should think the selections could not have been better made.

Believe me,
Yours sincerely,
A. C. SWINBURNE.

LETTER XCIII

To Thomas J. Wise

> *The Pines,*
> *Putney Hill,*
> *S.W.*
> *March 24th,* 1886.

Dear Mr. Wise,

I am very much obliged by the gift of your beautiful and curious reprint.[1] It is almost the only thing of Shelley's I never saw, and evidently of more characteristic value than many of his maturer and more elaborate prose writings.

Yours very truly,
A. C. Swinburne.

LETTER XCIV

To Edward Dowden

> *The Pines,*
> *Putney Hill,*
> *S.W.*
> *June 2nd,* 1886.

Dear Sir,

The late Lord Houghton bought the leaf containing Shelley's famous atheistic signa-

---

[1] *Review of Hogg's Memoirs of Prince Alexy Haimatoff. Edited by Thomas J. Wise.* London, 8vo, 1886.

ture in the album or book of inscriptions at the Chartreuse at Montauvert, and had it bound into a copy of one of Shelley's books—I think *The Revolt of Islam,* or it may have been *Laon and Cythna*—where he showed it to me, and whence I transcribed it. My impression is that there were no accents; but the blundering ω for ο was only too unmistakable. Lord Broughton's memory must have deceived him; for, of course, even if Shelley's signature and inscription might have been reproduced by forgery, the whole leaf—crammed on either side with entries of the regular tourist kind—could not have been.

Possibly Byron—whose itch for lying evidently amounted to a monomania—may have told Hobhouse that he had defaced the inscription, and Lord Broughton after so many years may have imagined that he had seen him do so. It was certainly later than 1860—not later, I think, than two or three years afterwards at most—that Mr. Milnes (as he then was) showed me the book containing the leaf cut out of the album.

Yours sincerely,
A. C. SWINBURNE.

LETTER XCV

To John Churton Collins

The Pines.
June 16th, 1886.

My dear Collins,

I ought to have thanked you long ago for your brilliant and interesting little book on Bolingbroke and Voltaire. The former, apart from his relations to Pope, has hitherto been little more to me than the shadow of a name; but Macaulay could not have made a more vivid and striking figure of him than you have done. I remember *old* Lord Lytton saying to me once in the course of conversation that of all men that ever lived he would like best to have been Lord Bolingbroke!!! If I thought the fancy an odd one then, I think it ten times odder now.

But I am particularly impelled to write to you just now because I want to express my cordial and delighted admiration (in which Watts desires me to tell you how heartily and thoroughly he shares) of your two invaluable papers on the educational crisis which appeared in *The Pall Mall Gazette* (pearls, I must take leave to say, on a dunghill) of May 28th and 31st. I never read anything with more absolute sympathy or with more sincere gratitude. I wish copies could be affixed to every door of the schools. The reasoning is unanswerable, and the expression unsurpassable.

> Ever yours truly,
> A. C. SWINBURNE.

LETTER XCVI

To Thomas J. Wise

> *The Pines,*
> *Putney Hill,*
> *S.W.*
> *June 23rd,* 1886.

Dear Mr. Wise,
Many thanks for your two little books. I wish the ugly and barbarous word "fac-simile" were abolished—Landor thought it only fit for the lips of printers' devils—and then there could be no discussion as to its proper use or meaning.

> Ever yours sincerely,
> A. C. SWINBURNE.

LETTER XCVII

To Richard Herne Shepherd

*The Pines,
Putney Hill,
July 3rd,* 1886.

DEAR MR. SHEPHERD,

Dr. John Brown's opinion is worth so much more than mine, that it seems to me quite superfluous for you to quote my letter; but certainly, if you think otherwise, I can have no objection to your doing so.

Thanks for the proofs.[1] The parody is amusing, as my memory assured me; but I wish Thackeray (if it be he) had not taken a subject so horribly disgusting to crack jokes upon. On the other hand, *Eugene Aram* is so provocative of ridicule that nothing (from that point of view) can be too strong or violent to be just or reasonable. Still, on reading it again, I am half sorry that this burlesque should be revived—though no doubt it is not wanting in cleverness of a rather coarse kind.

Yours very truly,
A. C. SWINBURNE.

[1] Of *Sultan Stork and Other Stories.*

LETTER XCVIII

To Thomas J. Wise

Leigh House,
Bradford-on-Avon,
Wilts.
July 15th, 1886.

DEAR MR. WISE,
    Of course anything I have written on the subject of Shelley is quite at your service, and the more use you may think fit to make of it the more gratified I shall be. Thanks for your pamphlet, and in anticipation for the *Epipsychidion,* which I am specially curious to see. I congratulate you on having discarded (in the term *"facsimile"*) a barbarous vulgarism, fit only—as Landor thought it—for printers' devils, and writers on the same level of culture and understanding as these.
    I remain,
        Yours very sincerely,
           A. C. SWINBURNE.

LETTER XCIX

To Edmund Gosse

The Pines,
October 27th, [18]86.

My dear Gosse,
Many thanks for your cordial note in acknowledgment of mine. I have now seen *The Quarterly Review,* and find, as I expected, that its malignity in this instance is, as usual, so glaring and palpable, so impudently and indecently naked, as to reduce the act of self-exposure to an act of suicide.

I did not even know that my name had had the honour to be insulted in any later number of that esteemed periodical than one of more than ten years ago, of which I never condescended to take any more direct notice than may seem to be conveyed in certain references on pages 27, 89, and 90 of my *Note on Charlotte Brontë,* where you will find my views expressed with all due moderation. I should be much obliged if you could tell me where to look for the attack on myself, as it could not but edify me to read, and I am out of reach of any public library where I might hunt it up.

You speak in one of your lectures of Mason's tragedy of *Muleasses* as having never, to your knowledge, attracted praise or notice from any quarter: but one very worthless tho' not very recondite authority—*The Biographia Dramatica*—has a flaming eulogy of its poetic merits tempered by a word of regretful condemnation on the "lowness" and "obscenity" of the comic parts—which are certainly rather strong in flavour. But I think the play on the whole, for all its bombast and all its bawdry, a fine tragic poem, worth all Cowley, Denham, and Waller—as far as I know their works—rolled together into one poeticule.

Ever sincerely yours,
A. C. SWINBURNE.

I need not add how happy I am to hear of the line taken by the Cambridge authorities

LETTER C

TO EDMUND GOSSE

The Pines,
October 29th, [18]86.

MY DEAR GOSSE,
I was just about to write to you when I opened this evening's *Athenæum* and found the answer to a question I meant to ask you as to the attack on myself. Can anything be funnier than the assumption of a writer in the *Quarterly,* the

Westminster, the *Edinburgh,* or any other Review which was of more or less note in the days of our fathers, that the authorship of an article in one of these organs must be known to persons who in fact were unaware of its existence? Alas, I have no claim to the credit so generously offered me for magnanimous forbearance, or condonation of an attack which, when I asked Watts if he had ever heard of, he replied that he thought you must be mistaken, as he could not have failed to hear of its existence, if existence it had. After that, I ask you, knowing as you do the extent of Watts's reading, whether an attack on literary grounds in the *Quarterly Review* is more serious, or worthier of notice in these days, than an attack on philosophic or speculative grounds in the *Church Times* or the *Record?*

But it was on a point better worth notice—if you think of vouchsafing any further notice to an anonymous attack—that I was going to address you. It seems to me that the most damaging single point made against you in the *Q. R.* article is the intimation—based on an unlucky ambiguous turn of phrase which does certainly lay itself open to malignant misconstruction—that you thought the *Arcadia* and the *Oceana* were poems. Now, on pages 322 and 323 of the *Q. R.* there is an oversight —not of the same kind, for it is infinitely graver— which in your place I certainly could not refrain from exposing to public ridicule. This classic champion thinks it interesting and profitable to compare the plays of SOPHOCLES and of Shakespeare (I should say few things were less profitable, but that of course is matter of opinion) and proceeds thus:—"How much, *for instance,* would a comparative study of *Macbeth* and *The Agamemnon,* of *Henry V.* and *The Persae* reveal?" Whence a reader, neither captious nor malevolent, might very naturally infer and very allowably assert that the reviewer believes *The Agamemnon* and *The Persae* to be the work of Sophocles.

After that, anything would be an anticlimax.

Ever sincerely yours,
A. C. SWINBURNE.

LETTER CI

To EDMUND GOSSE

The Pines.
November 13th, [18]86.

MY DEAR GOSSE,
Thank you for a very clever and amusing specimen of criticism by parody.[1] I think it most ingenious and excellent from the controversial point of view.

[1] By Professor A. W. Verrall, in *The Cambridge Review.*

I never did see Dennis on Milton, but I can most readily believe in his superiority to Addison on the same subject.

I have given your message to Watts.

And now, with regard to the "pirate" or malignant, I have only to request that you will wait till this day week, and then (if you look into *The Athenæum*) you will see what you will see. I did not think that our honourable and erudite friend [1] would have offered to "take it fighting"— his only chance being to "take it like a lamb, lying down," (I trust you know from what immortal classic I am quoting)—but as he tries or pretends to show fight, I have thought it worth while, (shall I say?) in a spirit of Christian love, to administer a moderate application—though certainly not quite so moderate as last week's too gentle dose— of salutary discipline.

Ever yours truly,
A. C. SWINBURNE.

[1] J. Churton Collins.

SWINBURNE'S LETTERS

LETTER CII

To Philip Bourke Marston

*The Pines,
Putney Hill,
S.W.
November 15th, 1886.*

My dear Philip,
    Some days ago I called Watts's attention to what struck me as the remarkable merit of some poems in a volume[1] I had lately received from the author,—poems which remind me, in some of their finer characteristics, rather of your own than of any other contemporary's. I am naturally much interested to hear of your connection with the author.

I thought "Absolution" certainly a powerful poem—perhaps as much in the style of Lee Hamilton's poems as of yours—very well conceived and constructed. I had read before (I forget where, but quite lately) "The Singing of the Magnificat," and it had struck me as something quite out of the common in conception. It is a pity the closing couplet should be so flat, but that might easily be remedied.

"Baby's Birthday" is a charming little piece, and

---

[1] *Lays and Legends.* By E. Nesbit.

I am rather fastidiously exacting with respect to poetry on the great subject of "Baby."

The first part of "Children's Playgrounds in the City" I like very much; and the whole of the poem called "The Dead to the Living" is powerfully pathetic.

Come and see me, if you can, on Friday next, and I will read you a lyric made near Beachy Head, while returning from a long walk thither. I am very much in love with Eastbourne—do you know it?

Ever sincerely yours,
A. C. SWINBURNE.

P.S.—I had forgotten to mention the poem called "Two Christmas Eves," which struck me as singularly powerful and original; the sort of poem that Charlotte Brontë might have written if she had had more mastery of the instrument of verse.

LETTER CIII

To Edward Dowden

The Pines,
Putney Hill,
S.W.
November 29th, 1886.

DEAR SIR,
I have just received the invaluable present announced on your postcard of the 25th, which

I did not at once acknowledge as I expected daily the arrival of the books, and did not like to write and say they had not come. I thank you most cordially for the gift. It is needless to say with what eagerness and pleasure I am reading—or with what earnestness and sincerity I congratulate you on having given to us all—the final and monumental life of Shelley.

While I think of it, I may observe that I do not think there can be any doubt as to the authenticity of the famous inscription shown me by the late Lord Houghton on the leaf of the Montauvert album, which he said he had purchased of the innkeepers and cut out of the book. You know the look of such leaves—the absurd aspect of fifty different scrawls on either side, interspersed with ejaculations and reflections—too frequently religious, and invariably sentimental (if not vulgar on the other branch line of vulgarity). If Shelley's inscription is forged, all the others on either side of the page must have been forged to match it! And why? There are no such blanks or gaps (unless a pretty good memory grossly deceives me) as would have afforded a forger the chance of an interpolation taking up so much space. As to the legend of the erasure of Shelley's inscription by a man more likely to have forged than to have erased an inscription likely to damage a friend, it must be remembered that if Hobhouse (who may have been as veracious as the run of mankind) affirmed it as a fact, it was also affirmed by Ananias Lord Byron, and it would need the solemn asseveration of twelve men (at least) of unblemished honour to prove the truth of anything asserted by that "liar of the first magnitude."

    Believe me,
     Very sincerely yours,
      A. C. SWINBURNE.

P.S.—I re-open this to add a small bibliographical note. Vol. II, p. 184, you put a query to the title *Martial Maid*. This is the sub-title of Fletcher's tragicomedy, *Love's Cure, or The Martial Maid*—a favourite of my own from early years for its boyish and high-spirited mixture of romance with burlesque.

LETTER CIV

To A. H. BULLEN

The Pines,
Putney Hill,
S.W.
February 12th, 1887.

MY DEAR SIR,
  I am very much obliged and gratified by the present of your beautiful book of *Songs*—

in a form worthy of the contents. It is a real "golden treasury" with no leaden admixture. And as gratitude is notoriously definable as a sense of future favours, how can I better express my gratitude than by the expression of a hope that John Marston may not have much longer to await his first edition—those hitherto so-called being non-edited?

You have done so much for the literature of the Shakespearean age, that the only appropriate or adequate recognition of our debt—of the obligation which all lovers and students of English poetry must always feel that they owe you—is to urge you to increase it.

Yours very sincerely,
A. C. SWINBURNE.

LETTER CV

To A. H. BULLEN

The Pines,
Putney Hill,
S.W.
May 1st, 1887.

MY DEAR SIR,

A thousand thanks for your beautiful and much needed edition of Marston. I have just had time to dip into your Introduction, which is full of interest. I myself think rather better of Marston's *Sophonisba* than you seem to do. The magnificent last words of the heroine have dwelt in my memory ever since I first read them (in Campbell's *Specimens*) at the advanced age of twelve. I think that scene one of the very grandest things in English poetry. That a man who could write tragic verse of such noble purity and simplicity should at other times premeditate such crabbed and barbarous bombast is alike irritating and inexplicable. I once had the pleasure of reading some of his finest scenes to my late dear friend Philip Marston,[1] the blind poet, who greatly admired and enjoyed the splendid work of his old namesake.

I must not forget to say how gratified I am by the honour you have done my opening words on the subject of our old dramatists, by prefixing them to your prospectus.

Believe me,
Yours very sincerely,
A. C. SWINBURNE.

P.S.—I notice a slight misprint on p. 121 (*v.* 418), of Vol. I.—"*aspish*" for "*apish.*" My copy, a cruelly cropped one, of the first Quarto reads "*apish.*" At p. 172, *v.* 22, I doubt the justice of

---

[1] Philip Bourke Marston (1850-1887), who had died on the 13th of February.

your reading, *"see"* for *"sir."* I need not remind you of what Dyce has a note on somewhere, the occasional occurrence of the apostrophe *"sir"* or *"sirs"* in a monologue.

P.P.S.—I wish you had taken Ben Jonson in hand before Beaumont and Fletcher; there seems to me far more need for a new complete and adequate edition of Ben, with all the various readings of the Quartos, etc., given at length for the first time in full.

One "more last" word. At p. 142 of Vol. I., second line, the word *"twelve"* (ejaculated by Antonio on hearing the clock strike) is wanted for the metre. At p. 150, *v.* 190, I would read—"to swell thy *honour* out,"—better sense and metre than *"hour"*?

LETTER CVI

To A. H. Bullen

The Pines,
Putney Hill,
S.W.
July 2nd, 1887.

My dear Sir,

I am bankrupt of thanks, though certainly not of thankfulness. I have received Nabbes[1] with much pleasure as I wish I could

[1] *The Works of Thomas Nabbes.* In two volumes. Edited by A. H. Bullen. Privately printed 1887.

express to you, and of course with corresponding gratitude.

Two of his plays, *Microcosmus* and *Tottenham Court,* I possessed in the old quartos, and they had made me wish to know the author better. What you say of the latter comedy expresses exactly what I felt when I had succeeded in picking or snapping up a copy, and was able to read further than the delightful and original opening which Lamb had made familiar to me ever since my thirteenth year. But on the whole I think it is a very good piece of work. The misfortune of any such Play as *Microcosmus* is that it cannot but remind one of the incomparable *Lingua,*[1] which I regard as one of the masterpieces of English literature. If the same man really wrote it and *The Country Girl,* it is a scandal that he should not be better known to his countrymen.

The Lovesick King, though certainly inferior, is a far from contemptible Play; indeed, taken on its own level, a really good one.

But I am writing about Brewer when I ought to be writing about Nabbes. Your severe verdict made me turn to *The Unfortunate Mother* to see if she were quite so unfortunate a daughter of the Muse of Nabbes; and I think you are very hard on her. The play is certainly not less readable

[1] A tragedy, by Anthony Brewer, printed in 1607. *The Country Girl* is of 1647, and *The Lovesick King* of 1655.

than many of Shirley's—who may (at his best, which is doubtless very good) be above the level of Nabbes, but certainly is not, I should say, in his average work.

Let me once more thank you, and congratulate you, on the splendid service you are doing to English letters.

Ever sincerely yours,
A. C. SWINBURNE.

LETTER CVII

To Edward Dowden

The Pines,
Putney Hill,
S.W.
September 27th, 1887.

MY DEAR SIR,
I hardly know whether I am more gratified to hear that you are about to edit Sir Henry Taylor's correspondence, or to hear that the letters which he addressed to me will make part of your selection. I am conscious that the letter which I naturally value the most, and treasure beyond well-nigh any other letter I ever received, that in which he speaks of my tragedy of *Mary Stuart,* is somewhat excessive in the magnificent generosity of its praise. But that consciousness is not enough

to deaden or to diminish my pleasure in the reflection that my work should have found such favour in the eyes of one English poet living in our time who could speak with authority on the subject of dramatic poetry.

As to my own letters addressed to so illustrious a correspondent, I have only to say that I shall be deeply gratified if they—or any part of them—should be considered worthy of preservation by the editor of Sir Henry's correspondence.

I am, dear Sir,
Yours very sincerely,
A. C. SWINBURNE.

LETTER CVIII

To A. H. BULLEN

The Pines,
Putney Hill,
S.W.
December 10th, 1887.

MY DEAR SIR,

I cannot thank you enough for your fresh gift of Lyrics from Elizabethan Song-books. But what I can express of thanks I must send at once. The cradle-song at p. 124 might be bound up with Blake's *Songs of Innocence*—and I know not what other poem might. But I see there is something on every leaf to enjoy and return thanks for. I have but my new volume to offer you—*not* in requital, but in acknowledgment.

An article of mine on your Marston, written some time since, will appear in *The Nineteenth Century* for February, I believe, and I hope you may like it.

Ever sincerely yours,
A. C. SWINBURNE.

LETTER CIX

To Thomas J. Wise

The Pines,
Putney Hill,
S.W.
April 25th, 1888.

DEAR MR. WISE,

I did not know that Hotten had republished, or reprinted, my stanzas on Sandys' drawing of *Cleopatra,* which appeared with an engraving of that fine drawing in *The Cornhill.* Mr. George Meredith, I remember, strongly (and no doubt justly) remonstrated with me for producing such a farrago of the most obvious commonplaces of my ordinary style as it was in 1866 or thereabouts. The verses were never intended for reproduction or preservation, but simply scribbled off as fast as might be to oblige a friend whose work I admired—just as in the preceding year I had written a few lines on his picture of "Spring," which appeared in *The Royal Academy Catalogue* of that year. I should no more have thought of reproducing the one improvisation than the other.[1]

My impression is that the best thing about *The Cornhill* poem was the motto—from an imaginary *Fall of Anthony* (1655). This was really a clipping from the first, undergraduate, sketch of *Chastelard*. If I were not a bit of a bibliomaniac myself, I should be shocked to think of your wasting good money on such a trumpery ephemeral.

Since I began this note your most interesting and valuable present has arrived.[2] Pray accept my cordial thanks for it.

Yours very sincerely,
A. C. SWINBURNE.

[1] The "friend" in question was Frederick Sandys, whose picture entitled "Gentle Spring" was exhibited in the Royal Academy Exhibition of 1865. Swinburne's "few lines," which appeared in *The Royal Academy Catalogue* for that year, p. 20, were never reproduced by him. They were included in *Posthumous Poems,* 1917.

The same *Catalogue* contained, upon p. 28, two stanzas of seven lines each, entitled "The Little White Girl," and signed *A. C. Swinburne.* The stanzas applied to the picture exhibited under that name by J. McN. Whistler. They were reprinted in the First Series of *Poems and Ballads,* 1866, as the fourth and sixth stanzas of "Before the Mirror."

[2] A copy of *Prologue to Hellas.* By Percy Bysshe Shelley. Now First Separately Printed. London: Printed for Private Circulation, 1886.

LETTER CX

To Thomas J. Wise

*The Pines,
Putney Hill,
S.W.
April 27th,* 1888.

DEAR MR. WISE,
    I am almost equally distressed and gratified by the extravagance of your kindness in sending me the little *Cleopatra*. I do not like to deprive you of what you thought worth—as you mentioned in your previous letter—a somewhat considerable price; considering that the most ardent bibliomaniac, if not a most outrageous egoist, draws the line at his own works. On the other hand, I cannot but value very highly such an evidence of good will, and such an example of generosity.

I am quite certain, quite positive, that I never set eyes on the booklet before, nor heard of its existence. It is to me a fresh proof that the moral character of the worthy Mr. Hotten was—I was about, very inaccurately, to say—ambiguous. He was a serviceable sort of fellow in his way, but decidedly what Dr. Johnson would have called "a shady lot," and Lord Chesterfield "a rum customer." When I heard that he had died of a surfeit of pork chops, I observed that this was a serious argument against my friend Sir Richard Burton's views of cannibalism as a wholesome and natural method of diet.

As to *Chastelard,* I began it—that is, I thought it out as a subject—at Oxford, and wrote possibly an Act or two before leaving, but nothing of it was ever printed till 1865; and then I had pretty thoroughly recast (not by any means cancelled) all the first and more boyish parts.[1]

As you may care to know, I may tell you that in the three numbers of the luckless *Undergraduate Papers* I published, as far as I remember, four "crudities," certainly no more: a paper on Marlow and Webster, some awful doggerel on the subject of *Tristram and Iseult,* a boyish bit of burlesque, and a terrific onslaught on the French Empire and its clerical supporters—which must no doubt have contributed in no inconsiderable degree to bring about its ultimate collapse. If ever you do see these worthless rarities, please remember that they were

[1] An ill fortune seems to have attended the original Manuscript of *Chastelard.* Much of it was destroyed; but other portions, after being returned by the printers, were again employed by the poet, the manuscript being crossed through, and fresh poems, etc., inscribed upon the blank versos of the pages.

Some of these fragments are happily still extant, and two at least of them have yielded matter of more than passing interest. Upon the back of one, formerly in the possession of Watts-Dunton, is written a list of the stories to be included in the projected *Triameron.*

literally a boy's work—legally an infant's. The article on the Dramatists, so far as I remember, was the only thing of any sort of value (except as showing a youngster's honest impulses and sympathies and antipathies)—and that I think I must have shown that before leaving Eton I had plunged as deep as a boy could dive into the line of literature which has always been my favourite. But when I think of the marvellous work that Rossetti (whose acquaintance I made just afterwards) had done at the same age, I am abashed at the recollection of my rubbish.

My friend Mr. Theodore Watts has asked me to ask you if copies of your wonderful facsimile of *The Masque of Anarchy* are procurable by non-members of the Shelley Society. I hope you will be able to tell me that they are.

By the way, I may as well warn you against putting trust in Mr. Shepherd's so-called *"Swinburniana."* Not only is the catalogue imperfect (I am speaking of the first issue), but it attributes to me—for one example—a poem which I should be glad (after a fashion) to have written, but which belongs, if I mistake not, to the date of King Henry VIII.[1] It was undertaken against my express

[1] *Dolorida,* printed in *Walnuts and Wine, A Christmas Annual,* 1883; and also by R. H. Shepherd in a double leaflet of four pages. The revival of this little poem greatly annoyed Swinburne, and in *The Pall Mall Gazette* for Dec. 28th, 1883, he emphatically denied his authorship of the verses. His

wish—but of course I have no right to complain of that—and as I positively though curtly refused to take any sort of cognizance of it, I cannot go into detail about its inaccuracies.

If you take in *The St. James's Gazette,* you will see that, like St. Paul, I have been fighting with beasts;[1] and I am up to my throat in Ben Jonson's undramatic works, of which I have undertaken to give an account simply because there is not a decently adequate one in existence.[2] I hope that on these accounts you will excuse a stupid, inadequate, long-winded, and egotistic letter—and will, in any case, believe me,

Very gratefully yours,
A. C. SWINBURNE.

I congratulate you upon the acquisition of *Sir Hugh the Heron*[3]—which is certainly something of a find. I should like to show you some of my rare books—not a large collection, but with a few very rare volumes in it; *e.g.* two of Boccaccio's

---

memory betrayed him; they *were* his, and in 1916 the original MS. in his writing turned up. He wrote them for the Album of Adah Isaacs Menken, in 1867.

[1] The reference is to Swinburne's Letters regarding Sir Henry Taylor, etc., which appeared in the *St. James's Gazette* for Monday, April 16th, 1888, and Tuesday, April 26th, 1888.

[2] Published in *The Nineteenth Century,* April and May, 1888; reprinted in *A Study of Ben Jonson,* 1889.

[3] *Sir Hugh the Heron, A Legendary Tale,* London, 1843. D. G. Rossetti's first book, printed privately by G. Polidori.

Latin Works, 1470 (a nice date?) printed in a character exactly, to my eyes, like *MS*. of the same period.

LETTER CXI

To Thomas J. Wise

*The Pines,
Putney Hills,
S.W.
May 2nd,* 1888.

Dear Mr. Wise,

Can you come to luncheon next Monday at half-past one? If another day would suit you better, any one except Sunday would suit me equally well.

The Boccaccio Folio is not *the* rarest rarity I can show you. That is an English black-letter book (a family heirloom in its way) which I fear must be unique. I would gladly forego the value of an unique possession to know that there was a perfect copy anywhere. I think there must have been a copy in the nursery of Mr. John Shakespeare's house, and that his little boy must have been in very early days much impressed by the drawings which represent, and the verses which describe, the ten—not seven—ages of man. Alas, both are imperfect! Many generations of small fingers have torn and worn away both ends of the leaf; but what remains is priceless. I am afraid it may, or must, be unique, for I have asked both Bodleian and British Museum authorities, if I rightly remember, and no one has ever seen another copy.

About modern rarities—unless the rare impression contains something unprocurable—I am so indifferent that it would be a sin and a shame for me to deprive you of your *Cleopatra*. Seven guineas! Heaven and Earth! It would have been dear at as many shillings and not cheap at as many pence. Wordsworth and Shelley, and Landor of course, are the only moderns whose first editions I care for, and I have got all I care for of Shelley's. Dr. Grosart lent me for a day the black tulip of that sort of book—the *very* first edition of *Lyrical Ballads*, containing the never republished "Convict."[1] I do break the tenth commandment into shivers when I think of that book! I have got the 1800 edition of it, but that curious imitation of Cowper, a bit of regular eighteenth century conventualism to sentiment and metre and expression, was even then cancelled.

I need hardly say that I know nothing, and never

[1] *The Convict ("The glory of evening was spread through the west")*, published in the First Edition of the *Lyrical Ballads*, 1798. This poem, in which Wordsworth advocated transportation as a substitute for the gallows, was never reprinted during the poet's lifetime. Mr. Hutchinson suggests that it was probably composed as early as 1793.

heard of it till now, of any such volume as you mention published or printed by Hotten under my name. And I certainly never wrote a poem, though I certainly did once write a ghost story, called *Dead Love*—till 1883 (*Roundels*)—and that I did not remember till this minute.

Mr. Watts desires me to send you his thanks for the promised copy of *The Masque of Anarchy,* which he will greatly value.

When you come—as I trust you will on Monday—remind me to show you the first book (in boards) and the first pamphlet (in sheets) printed or published by Landor in 1795;[1] and the little volume of his Latin Idyls printed at Oxford, of which the existence had been disbelieved—nay, denied, I think—even by his biographers. I have picked up two copies, and one of them I gave to the Master of Balliol.[2] But I have not the first and inaccurate edition of *Gebir* (1799),—only the revised one of 1800, with the misprints corrected. It is

---

[1] "The first book in boards"—Landor's *Poems* of 1795; the first pamphlet in sheets—the *Moral Epistle to Earl Stanhope,* 1795. These two books were in immaculate condition, and at Swinburne's request Mr. Wise had them fitted by Zaehnsdorf with fire-proof levant cases. After the poet's death these two volumes, rendered additionally delightful by their association with the author of *Atalanta* and *Hertha,* passed into the possession of Mr. Wise.

[2] *Idyllia Nova Quinque Heroum Atque Heroidum,* Oxford, 1815. Swinburne's second copy he retained until his death, when it also was acquired by Mr. Wise.

curious—in 1888—to think that in 1864 I sat and talked with the author!

Yours very sincerely,
A. C. SWINBURNE.

LETTER CXII

To A. H. Bullen

<i>The Pines,
Putney Hill,
S.W.
May 16th,</i> [1888].</div>

My dear Sir,
    I am sorry to hear that you are spending any part of your valuable time on Horace, or any one who may have wasted any part of his in translating that writer. I should as soon think of doing Moore into Greek anapaests, or Tupper into Greek elegiacs (I fancy he would read like Theognis or Tyrtaeus) as of turning Horace into English. My dislike of him—dating from schooldays—is one of the very few points on which I find myself in sympathy with Byron.

I do hope this undertaking of yours will not retard your promised edition of Davenport. You have done so much service to English letters by your devotion to our own great forgotten writers, that I cannot but grudge the expenditure of your industry and ability on less valuable matters.

I wish you would give us a reprint of the play so powerfully recommended by Ben Jonson—*Cynthia's Revenge*. I have seen it at the British Museum, but never read it through. It *cannot* be such rubbish as another play commended by Ben's unscrupulous good nature, *The Shepherd's Holiday*;[1] but even if it were, one would like to have the evidence.

Yours sincerely,
A. C. SWINBURNE.

LETTER CXIII

To A. H. BULLEN

<i>The Pines,
Putney Hill,
S.W.
July 27th,</i> 188</div>

MY DEAR SIR,

I have just received William Bullein's *Dialogue*, and begun gathering some of the numberless plums in it at random. As it is of course to your kindness that I owe this as well as so many other valued or rather invaluable gifts, I must send you my most grateful and cordial acknowledgments at once. I have unfortunately—and stupidly—mislaid your address since I last wrote,

---

[1] A Pastoral, 1629, by Walter Montague.

and I never can remember anyone's—not always my own; so I have to send this word of acknowledgment to your publishers. I hope this will not delay the arrival of my thanks longer than a day or two at most.

Have you observed the coincidence between the delightful "Tale of a Frier and his Boy," in your note at pp. 68–70, and Browning's "Pietro of Albano?" It struck me the moment I read this passage—which, I should have thought, would have have been worthy of a place in the text. But I must suppose you had good reason for preferring to reprint the later edition.

What an admirable writer, narrator, and humourist this old namesake of yours seems to have been! I have been very busy of late, but I look forward to a speedy improvement of my acquaintance with him.

Yours very sincerely,
A. C. SWINBURNE.

P.S.—Can you let me know whether copies of this book can be bought by non-subscribers, and at what price?

LETTER CXIV

To A. H. Bullen

The Pines,
Putney Hill,
S.W.
August 14th, 1888.

MY DEAR SIR,

I fear you have been thinking me the most thankless and discourteous of men to have been so long in acknowledging your kind offer. My excuse must be that I have written no letters whatever since the 5th, being almost incapable of letter-writing when I have other work on hand. The sincerity of my thanks must serve, if possible, as an apology for their tardiness.

I should, of course, be very grateful for the half-dozen copies of W. Bullein's *Dialogue* which you so kindly propose to send me; and the friends among whom they would be distributed would be worthy of so valuable a gift and so delightful a book.

Your sincerely,
A. C. SWINBURNE.

I send you, as some small return, a poem [1] which

[1] *The Armada.*

you may probably not have seen—unless you take in the *Fortnightly* at Dalkeith.

LETTER CXV

To Sir Sidney Lee

*The Pines,
Putney Hill,
S.W.
August 15th,* 1888.

Dear Sir,
　　I have no objection to my name being added to those already appearing on the committee,[1] but I could not undertake to attend any meetings or take any active part in its proceedings. It is very difficult to suggest what form such a memorial shall take; but, as you do me the honour to apply to me for an opinion on the subject, I may say that any form of tribute to so great and so glorious a memory as that of the first tragic poet of England must be better, at this late date, than none. The lamentable absence, not only of any portrait, but of any record—so far as I know—of Marlowe's likeness, makes it of course impossible to realize the wish I expressed thirteen years ago to see a statue raised to his memory—unless we

---

[1] For erecting a monument to Christopher Marlowe at Canterbury.

had a Michel Angelo to conceive and realize it. If subscriptions enough could be got, I should think nothing could be so appropriate as a series of medallions representing the principal figures of his work; Faustus with his good and evil angel, Hero and Leander, Tamburlaine,

"Like his desire, lift upwards and divine."

(a verse which always suggests to me the ideal likeness of Marlowe himself), Barabbas and Mephistopheles as devils or grotesques among the heroes and heroines, Edward and Gaveston, Mortimer and Isabella, and possibly others. I cannot guess whether this would be at all feasible; probably not; but I send it for what it may be worth—presumably *nil*.

Yours very truly,
A. C. S<small>WINBURNE</small>.

LETTER CXVI

T<small>O</small> A. H. B<small>ULLEN</small>

*The Pines,
Putney Hill,
S.W.
August 25th*, 1888.

M<small>Y</small> <small>DEAR</small> S<small>IR</small>,
The best way of thanking you for the splendid present of six copies of the delightful

Dialogue should be to tell you how much pleasure they have already given to me and to others. I have only yet given away two, but you may be sure they are thoroughly appreciated.

I am pleased to know that you took pleasure in reading my "Armada." But of course you know that the glorious verse or verses—

> *They shall ride*
> *Over ocean wide*
> *With hempen bridle and horse of tree—*

are of unknown antiquity, and that I only ventured to turn them into one verse and take that as the key-note of a new metre.

As to the Irish question, though I hope I may say that no living writer (to say the least) has shown more abhorrence of cruelty and tyranny than I have, I must say that, considering the age, and the treatment of "heretics" and "rebels" in every other kingdom, I feel a certain inclination to smile when I hear the severities inflicted on Ireland by the government of Elizabeth or Cromwell made the subject of shrieking and wailing. I fancy if you were to read the record of the "dragonnades"—of the horrors inflicted, without any shadow of provocation or any pretence of rebellion, on people who merely asked to be allowed to worship in their own way—and did not, like the modern Irish, enforce their demand by the practice of the basest and most barbarous atrocities—you would find something much more heart-rending than the record of English cruelties in Ireland; at least I have never heard that the English "rolled mothers with children down the rocks," because they refused to accept the reformed religion.

With renewed thanks,
Believe me,
Very sincerely yours,
A. C. SWINBURNE.

LETTER CXVII

To A. H. Bullen

2, The Terrace,
Lancing-on-Sea,
Sussex.
October 18th, 1888.

MY DEAR SIR,

The above address must plead my excuse for seemingly thankless delay in acknowledging the arrival of your last and not least beautiful anthology. It has just been forwarded hither from Putney, and I hasten to send you my tardy but most sincere thanks. The love-verses seem all delightful in their several ways of fancy, or of feeling, or of fun. The Raleigh poem is most interesting and valuable.

I am very glad to know that you like my article

on Marston. It was written last year on the appearance of your edition, and I cannot of course guess why its publication was so long deferred by the Editor of *The N[ineteenth] C[entury]* as to coincide, quaintly enough, with the appearance in *The Fortnightly* of my paper on Ben Jonson's *Discoveries*.

I am very glad to hear of the new popular edition of your *Lyrics*.

Ever sincerely yours,
A. C. SWINBURNE.

LETTER CXVIII

To Sir Sidney Lee

The Pines.
November 5th, 1888.

MY DEAR SIR,

I should say, by all means, Canterbury. I am glad that the idea of placing the memorial at Deptford has been abandoned, and very glad that Mr. Halliwell-Phillipps is of the same opinion as I am—or rather, I should say, that I have the honour of seconding the opinion of so illustrious a scholar on a subject of such peculiar interest, and one on which his opinion is of such exceptional value.

I could not possibly attend the proposed meeting on Thursday, but I am happy to hear of it, and sincerely gratified that my view should be found worthy of consideration.

    I am,
     Yours very truly,
      A. C. SWINBURNE.

LETTER CXIX

To Sir Sidney Lee

The Pines.
December 13*th,* 1888.

DEAR SIR,
   I can only repeat what I said before, that Canterbury is not merely the best, but the only proper site (in my humble opinion) for a memorial to Marlowe. Even if the Dean would subscribe—instead of demanding—£250 for the erection of a monument to his memory in Westminster Abbey, I should continue to think that it was not the place for such a monument. A so-called "poets' corner" where Shakespeare, Milton and Shelley "shine by their absence" is surely not the place for Marlowe. There is every reason why Canterbury should enjoy the honour which I am delighted to hear that it "is anxious for." And, I may be allowed to add, I think they are quite right in wishing that the site should not be in the cathedral. One of the most eminent Englishmen (and clergymen) living once

expressed to me his regret that the doors of the Abbey should have been closed against Byron. I replied that I thought it much more discreditable that Shelley should not have his place there. "Ah," was the answer, "but think how he would have disliked it!" Would Marlowe have disliked it less? Giordano Bruno, I see in to-day's papers, is to have his statue in Rome—but not in St. Peter's.

I saw the tribute paid to Marlowe by an anonymous and presumably illegitimate descendant and representative of the Puritan libeller who was "happily hanged" at Tyburn. *The Dunghill Gazette,* whose editor has served his term as a criminal in gaol for an act of unmentionable obscenity and infamy—committed, of course, in the interest of Social Purity—is exactly the organ in which such a protest should have appeared.

I will think over your suggestion that I should write something about our scheme for doing honour to Marlowe—but really I have written (I am glad and proud to remember it)—so many pages of prose and verse in his praise that I doubt if I could find anything fresh to say.[1]

Yours very truly,
A. C. SWINBURNE.

[1] Swinburne eventually wrote *Inscriptions for four sides of a Pedestal,* each consisting of one six-line stanza. They are to be found in *Astrophel and Other Poems,* 1894, pp. 121-122, but not upon the monument at Canterbury.

LETTER CXX

To A. H. Bullen

The Pines,
Putney Hill,
S.W.
December 16th, 1888.

MY DEAR SIR,

I must congratulate you as cordially as I thank you. In issuing the first edition of Campion's *Works* you have added a name to the roll of English poets, and one that can never be henceforward overlooked or erased. Certainly his long neglected ghost ought now to be rejoicing in Elysium.

I hope you have not forgot that Davenport and William (not to speak of Samuel) Rowley are still awaiting the honour you have done to Nabbes; that they will not have to wait much longer I may be allowed also to express a hope. Also I do trust you will think of Heywood and Dekker before Shirley, or even Beaumont and Fletcher. These—and I might add Chapman—need so much more urgently the help of your invaluable and indefatigable devotion.

Ever gratefully and sincerely yours,
A. C. SWINBURNE.

LETTER CXXI

To A. H. Bullen

*The Pines,
Putney Hill,
S.W.
November 24th,* 1889.

MY DEAR SIR,
   I have once more to thank you for a most beautiful and valued gift. Your volume of *Lyrics from the Dramatists* is worthy to stand beside its predecessors—and what praise could possibly be higher?

Yours very gratefully,
A. C. SWINBURNE.

P.S.—My friend Mr. Watts is anxious to know whether a large paper copy of this book is still to be had. Might I ask you to let me know?

I also am anxious—to know that we may hope before *very* long for a Rowley or a Davenport such as you alone can give us. These two noble if unequal writers have waited so *very* long for a further instalment of the justice first done them by Lamb; and in Davenport's case Washington Irving!

There is a charming bridal song in Nat. Lee's

SWINBURNE'S LETTERS

Cæsar Borgia,[1] which I wish you had included in this volume. It is worth a shoal of Davenport's, and would hold its own among Fletcher's. One can hardly believe the evidence of fact that it is a production of the age of Dryden. I want to get poor Lee his share of credit; but was ever man born under such an evil star? Its effect eclipses and obscures him even yet.

LETTER CXXII

To Messrs. Smith, Elder & Co.

*The Pines,
Putney Hill,
S.W.
December 29th,* 1889.

DEAR SIRS,

I regret that it is impossible for me to attend the funeral of the illustrious man [2] who is to be interred on Tuesday. Therefore I return,

---

[1] It may be worth noting that the hero of this play (1680) is that Duke of Gandia whom Swinburne was now proposing to make the subject of a tragedy of his own. The "charming bridal song" is that in Scene 1 of Act IV.:—

*Grasp the pleasure while 'tis coming,
Though your beauties now are blooming;
Time at last your joys will sever,
And they'll part, they'll part for ever.*

[2] Robert Browning.

with most sincere acknowledgments, the ticket you were good enough to send me.
> Yours very faithfully,
> A. C. SWINBURNE.

LETTER CXXIII

To A. H. BULLEN

> *The Pines,*
> *Putney Hill,*
> *S.W.*
> *May* 19*th*, 1890.

MY DEAR SIR,
    I have already been asked to write something to be spoken on the occasion of the performance to which you allude, and have declined to do so, thinking that I have already said what I have to say on the subject.

When are you going to add to our many obligations by giving us a first edition of Davenport? I am eager to possess his complete works.
> Yours sincerely,
> A. C. SWINBURNE.

LETTER CXXIV
To A. H. Bullen

*The Pines,
Putney Hill,
S.W.*
October 10*th,* 1890.

MY DEAR SIR,

I cannot thank you enough for the gift of *Davenport*. I have been longing for years to possess his works (having only the *C[ity] N[ightcap]* and *J[ohn] and M[atilda]*, in 4to, especially since reading *A New Trick [to Cheat the Devil]* in the Bodleian). I hope the next of your invaluable services to the study of English poetry and drama will be the first edition of Rowley.

With sincere congratulations,
Yours most gratefully,
A. C. SWINBURNE.

LETTER CXXV
To A. H. Bullen

*The Pines,
Putney Hill,
S.W.*
November 10*th,* 1890.

MY DEAR SIR,

I must send one word of apologetic explanation to follow my former note of thanks. My article in *The Fortnightly* would have been a good deal longer, and the tribute of thanks and recognition to you would have been much fuller and less inadequate, if I had not been so pressed for time that I had to count not by hours but by minutes the time left me to conclude it, if it was to appear this month—as of course I wished it should, in order that some little acknowledgment might appear in print while your *Davenport* was still a new book. I had to sacrifice the full expression of my gratitude to the desire of expressing some part of it betimes; but I hope you will agree with my estimate of your author on the whole, and believe that nothing but pressure of time could so have curtailed my acknowledgment of our obligation to you,—and especially of the more especial obligation due from

Yours most sincerely,
A. C. SWINBURNE.

LETTER CXXVI

To A. H. Bullen

The Pines,
Putney Hill,
S.W.
December 24th, 1890.

MY DEAR SIR,

Many thanks for your beautiful edition of an old friend's *Poetical Rhapsody*. I am only sorry that your priceless labours in this delightful line are at an end; but I hope, as I have said (I believe) when thanking you for *Davenport,* that you will be able before long to make us even more your debtors by the gift of a first edition of *Rowley.*

You will probably have seen in *The Fortnightly Review* for November the article in which—when greatly pressed for time—I tried to express my estimate of Davenport, and my gratitude to his editor.

With all good wishes for the Christmas season,
Ever sincerely yours,
A. C. SWINBURNE.

LETTER CXXVII

To FRANCIS WARRE CORNISH

The Pines.
March 14th, '91.

MY DEAR SIR,
I ought to have thanked you by return of post for your gratifying reception of my little ode [1] or odelet, and also for the copy of verse which I am sending on to a friend who will be interested to see them, and (I think) pleased to find that Eton

[1] *Eton: an Ode,* printed in the *Athenæum* for May 30, 1891, and reprinted in *Astrophel and Other Poems,* 1894, pp. 110-113.

has not so wholly changed her skin since our time as to have utterly forsaken the poor old Muses for more fashionable objects of cult.

I am glad you approve of my reference to Shelley, whom I naturally regard—*ut Etoniæ loquar*—as in some respects my major: so I determined, as soon as I made up my mind to undertake this task, that at all events I would throw his name in the teeth of the orthodox who believe in that one rather small God, Gray.

Believe me,
Very sincerely yours,
A. C. SWINBURNE.

LETTER CXXVIII

To Theodore Watts–Dunton

August 25th, 1891.

MY DEAR WALTER,

I am so sleepy to-day I cannot see out of my eyes after so many hours of walking and scrambling yesterday as might have tired out any boy but Bertie, and such hard scrambling too as I never, or hardly ever, underwent since I "played truant" at his age, or younger. I lost my way hopelessly among the hills, and had to wade, climb, grope, fight, jump, writhe, crawl, and flounder through woods, briars, morasses, thickets, hedges, ravines, glades, gorges and galleys without number before regaining (as an Irishman might say) the wrong road—and such a road! It *may* have been mended (though I doubt it) by order of the Board of Druids or Boadicæa—but assuredly never since; and its original angle—now a good deal sharper— may have been but little more acute than this

W V E

Vale of Evesham

The high roads have a humorous habit of vanishing, or turning into demented sheeptracks, left incomplete by an inebriated shepherd after his first bemused and zigzagging attempt at primitive or troglodytic road-making. The woods and lawns are lovely to the northward; but the whole country-side is waterless, but for occasional quagmires and a rare and curious puddle once in ten miles or so. I need not add that I am beginning to like the country very much.

In the evening I read to Charlotte and Isobel, what book do you guess? *Tristram Shandy*. They can talk of nothing else, and are (like me) almost as fond of Mr. Shandy as of Uncle Toby. *A propos,* I am certain the Oxmoor must be in this neighbourhood. As I say, my mother would have been such a much better helpmate for him than Tristram's; she would so thoroughly have entered into his views on Christian names, in which we none of us see anything to smile at.

I am very grateful for your great kindness in trying to see Knowles about my poem, and very Shandically disappointed at its non-appearance in large type at the head of a magazine with everything handsome about it.

I see my mother now daily, and she continues to do well—took medicine yesterday, but had a good night.

Kind regards from us all.

Ever yours,
A. C. SWINBURNE.

LETTER CXXIX

To Sir E. Burne-Jones

The Pines.
October 15th, 1892.

MY DEAR NED,

How am I to thank you for the sweetest photograph ever taken? Watts and I are now Palamon and Arcite, our hitherto impregnable friendship breached and shattered by rivalry in devotion to the lady whose adorable arm (what can the missing arms of the Venus of Milo's have been to that one) is caressing your honoured beard.

When will you come? or would you prefer luncheon or dinner time? Give it a name I beg. And do not be tempted to put off. Remember how many souls which Almighty God designed for salvation have been eternally lost thro' the apparently venial sin of procrastination.

I am awfully sorry and taken aback (*erasures*) ... As for being old I can only say in language appropriate to our time of life that I like your something cheek. We ought all, like Hugo and Tennyson, at our time of life to have many of our best years before us. I should rather think you did not see me at the Abbey on Wednesday, I sent back my card with a word of excuse just as I did when I received one for the funeral of Browning. I hate all crowds and all functions, but especially the funereal kind beyond all decent expression. But I did write a little word to Lady Tennyson, having once been their guest, which I am glad to know was found acceptable.

I want you to like an unpublished poem of mine which has been very successful in MS. and which I should have liked to send Tennyson (but Omnipotence overruled our humble aspirations! as I need not remind you) on my countrywoman Grace Darling. I went with dear old Scott who was hideously sick all the way out from Joyous Gard to the lighthouse, where the heroine's old father who had rescued the shipwrecked crew from off the rocks while she kept the boat steady to take them in received us. Didn't you ever when a boy think how you would like of all things to keep or live in a lighthouse? I do to this day. Of course I mean if it's some miles out to sea and difficult to get at. Isn't the name of our Northumbrian reefs about that one lovely—The Hawkers. Falconers and falcons with ships and men for prey instead of herons (I always thought it rather a shame to hawk at them—they are so beautiful, especially, *of course,* in Northumberland).

I hope you got all right, I fear you may not have had time to read my little book of this year: *The Sisters.* It found less favour with the reviewer than with my mother, whose chief criticism was, "I like Redgie so much," which gave me more pleasure than any review could as I did think I had succeeded in making a nice young fellow out of my own recollections and aspirations. On getting into one's teens, a little way—the cavalry service is apt to supplant even the keeping of a lighthouse in one's fancy, or may I be allowed the endearing word Ideal. I hope you will not be bored by this prolonged scrawl, but the man to whom the absence and the silence of an honoured friend has been for many, many revolutions of the lunar globe an affliction (grammarians not unaware would say that they had been afflictions—

but what, my dearest sir, is grammar to sentiment?), may be forgiven if he adds no further expression of apology for excessive and unpremeditated verbosity in addressing a friend
by his very devoted
A. C. SWINBURNE.

LETTER CXXX

To WILLIAM POEL

The Pines,
Putney Hill, S.W.
October 27th, 1892.

MY DEAR SIR,

I must send you a word of thanks for the honour done me as a Websterian by your gift of a box on the 25th, and for the great pleasure I had in seeing that transcendent masterpiece of tragedy [1] restored to the stage under such favourable auspices. How great that pleasure was, you may judge when I tell you that I was just twelve years old when I first read so much of "The Duchess" as is given in Campbell's "Specimens," and was as much entranced and fascinated at that,

---

[1] Webster's *Duchess of Malfy*, performed by the Elizabethan Stage Society. For this revival Swinburne wrote a Prologue, printed first in *The Nineteenth Century,* and afterwards included in *A Channel Passage and Other Poems,* 1904, pp. 188-189.

not very mature, age, as I am now, and have been ever since by its unique beauty and power.

I congratulate you most cordially on the benefit you have conferred upon all lovers of English dramatic poetry at its best and highest, in other words, upon all lovers of what is best and highest in the literature, or rather in the creative work of all countries and all ages. And I most earnestly hope that you may see your way to doing as much for other great works of the same great age, especially, I need not say, of the same great hand. I think I must have been the only person present on Tuesday who had brought with him a copy of the author's edition (1623). I wish I had had the privilege of shewing you the beautiful little quarto which I had slipped into an inside breast pocket. But I hope you may be kind enough to allow me an opportunity of shewing you my little collection of such rarities. It would be no sort of return for your kindness, but it would be a great pleasure for me and might, I think, be of some interest to you.

Believe me, in the meantime,
Yours very gratefully,
A. C. SWINBURNE.

LETTER CXXXI

To Edmund Gosse

The Pines,
Putney Hill,
London.
November 1st, [18]92.

My dear Gosse,
    Many thanks for your beautiful little volume. I have read *Jack* in Grosart's edition with considerable interest; indeed, I read the whole of Nash's works through from the first line to the last. Your preface is full of interest and of excellent criticism. I myself like the "breathless" style (as you very happily describe it) of *Pierce Pennilesse* better than you seem to do—that is, in its way, which I do not find wearisome in such strong hands as Nash's.

I am amused to find that the work[1] which virtuous hands tore to pieces is still extant in MS. Has it any merit? It ought to be privately reprinted, in any case, if only on account of the authorship. It can't be worse than "that good man Stead's" published receipts of what Middleton calls "An artificial maid, a doctored virgin."[2]

[1] Nash's *The Choice of Valentines,* first printed by J. S. Farmer, in 1899.
[2] This refers to Stead's articles entitled *The Maiden Tribute of Modern Babylon* contributed to *The Pall Mall Gazette.*

When are you coming to look us up? Watts unites with me in this inquiry, and we both hope that it may soon be practically answered.

Please give my kindest regards to Mrs. Gosse, and believe me,

Ever sincerely yours,
A. C. SWINBURNE.

LETTER CXXXII

To Edmund Gosse

Near the South-Western Railway Station. N.B. [This is not my direction but Watts's—I have had to borrow his paper.]

The Pines, Putney Hill, London. November 14*th*, [18]92.

MY DEAR GOSSE,
                I should have thanked you for your letter before now but for the impediment of a half-disabled right hand (wrist sprained and small bones at the back of it all strained by a fall: till the dense loose carpet of miry wet leaves was cleared away, to come down this hill after sunset was really dangerous last week). Davies of Hereford and Dr. Grosart—I wish he would reissue *The Scourge of Folly* separately—(do you know

---

Upon this subject Swinburne wrote *Holy Paris,* and a series of *Rondeaux Parisiens,* which were privately printed in 1917.

his present address, which I have mislaid?) had made me acquainted with the admirably frank, simple, and suggestive title of Master Tom's missing poem. (What cheek! as a schoolboy should say. I suppose he had been studying the "Divino" Aretino.) By all means let us have the text, however corrupt, and then try whether a new Bentley may not be found to do as much for it as Mr. Ellis has done for Catullus (I *don't* mean translate it into Latin, but rectify metrical and other defects). The metre must be very curious, and what you say of its "force and picturesqueness" would be enough to make it, in my opinion, not only "right," but a duty to preserve such a curious relic of so distinguished and interesting a man of genius as Nash —seeing that he thought fit not merely to write, but (as I understand) to publish it.

I am up to my ears and over them in a "Study" of Heywood. Do you think he did write *The Trial of Chivalry* and not *Dick of Devonshire?* I fancy he "had a main finger" in both.

With kindest remembrances from Watts and myself to Mrs. Gosse and yourself, and joint hopes to see you here before long.

Ever sincerely yours,
A. C. SWINBURNE.

LETTER CXXXIII

To Edmund Gosse

The Pines.
November 24th, [1892].

My dear Gosse,
 I must begin by answering your postscript with a thousand thanks for it. I should think I *did* remember the best friend of my schoolboy-hood! It is a very great pleasure to hear again of Sir George Young after such a lifetime of years, and to find that he remembers our old communion in dramatic poetry (I cared for nothing else in those days). Examine him in *The Revenger's Tragedy,* and tell me what he remembers of that refreshing and rose-tinted work of genius— tho' I remember (with grief) that you are a blasphemous heretic about Cyril Tourneur, whom I have always honoured ever since I was in my earliest teens. Please remember me to him (not Cyril, but Sir G.) most particularly.

What do you think about *The Trial of Chivalry?* I take it to be one of the plays that Heywood "had a finger" in. Not very good—but might have been.

How very curious is all that you tell me about Nash's poem! It must be an unique instance of the survival of a murdered book. I suppose there is really no doubt that it was printed, published, and destroyed by episcopal order? One would have expected that one or two printed copies might or must have escaped—but the existence of two or three manuscripts is really too odd—and comic. It would be hard if collation could not supply a perfect text. If it does, I will write a congratulatory ode to the beatified spirit of Tom in the Elysian fields—and it shall be in the favourite metre of Aristophanes, who was (I believe) the first poet, as far as we know, to celebrate or to mention in verse the serviceable and interesting implement of feminine toilette to which Tom devoted a whole poem.

With kindest remembrances to Mrs. Gosse and yourself,

Ever sincerely yours,
A. C. SWINBURNE.

LETTER CXXXIV

TO EDMUND GOSSE

The Pines.
December 5th, [18]92.

MY DEAR GOSSE,

I return Sir G. Young's letter with many thanks.

I don't know when my *Heywood* will be finished; so many other things have come in the way of it that I begin to doubt whether it will be ready A.D. 1900. As to the book comprising all my studies of the Shakespearean age, I hope to have it ready for the press when I find myself nearer 80 than 70. But then it will be *the* book on the subject, done once for all and never to be superseded.

As for that miserable old miscreant "Scotus,"[1] you have already seen by this time what justice I have done upon him. . . . I have plucked his ghost out of Lethe, and chucked it into Tartarus.

I am glad to find you orthodox about Tourneur —but surely you were once a blasphemer? Of course no mortal thinks of him as existing outside the range of tragic drama—but there he holds his own high, narrow little fortress (like one of our Border "peels," if you know what they are) apart from all others and inexpugnable by any.

With all kind messages to all of you,
Ever sincerely yours,
A. C. SWINBURNE.

[1] William Bell Scott, whose posthumous memoirs had just appeared.

LETTER CXXXV

To Edward Dowden

> The Pines,
> Putney Hill,
> S.W.
> [*March,* 1893.]

Dear Mr. Dowden,
You must have thought me shamefully remiss in acknowledging the honour done me by your letter of the 23rd of last month. My excuse must be that I did not like to answer it without sending you the song which I have only this very day been able to work up into a form that at all satisfied me—having been hindered from work first by illness of my own, and then by anxiety about my mother. This spring has been as treacherously constant to inconstancy as if the dispenser were named Gladstone.

I have tried to make the song[1] as simple, straightforward, and easily singable as I could; and you will see that I have been mindful of your desire that it should be "a song for Irish Unionists—not exclusively Ulster men." If there is anything you could wish—for any reason—at all differently expressed, my verses shall for once be even

[1] *The Union,* printed in *The Nineteenth Century* for May 1893, and reprinted in *Astrophel and Other Poems,* 1894, pp. 114-116.

as the principles dearest to the heart and most sacred to the conscience of Mr. Gladstone; in other words—the proverbial words of a more honest transatlantic Gladstone, who was evidently not "a pure Scotchman"—if you do not like them, they can be altered.

Very truly yours,
A. C. SWINBURNE.

LETTER CXXXVI

To Thomas J. Wise

The Pines,
Putney Hill,
S.W.
April 3rd, 1893.

DEAR MR. WISE,

You must have wondered at receiving no thanks for your note of the 22nd, and the volume accompanying it. My excuse must be a passing attack of influenza, and the subsequent lassitude, hardly yet shaken off. Accept my thanks for both.

The day before they arrived I had seen with delight the printed announcement of the recovered *Simonidea*.[1] I have many (and have alas! had

---

[1] Landor's *Simonidea, Bath, Printed by W. Meyler* [1806]. For many years *Simonidea* had been practically impossible of acquisition, the only perfect copy then known to exist being in the Forster Library, at South Kensington Museum. A

more) Landorian rarities; but this blue diamond, black tulip, or roc's egg, I had reluctantly given up all hope of ever seeing.

Are you beneficent enough to think of having it reprinted? The very thought makes me feel inclined to "drop into poetry" and perpetrate a song of gratulation and thanksgiving—I was about to say a Sonnet, but I remember the old master's eccentric hatred of that inoffensive form of verse.

Nothing could give me more pleasure than a visit from you, and Mr. Watts desires me to join the expression of his wish and hope for it to mine. I am sorry to say he is now the invalid, but will, I hope, soon be all right again. I ought to have written before now in his name as well as my own; but you must accept, in both our names, my foregoing explanation and apology.

Ever sincerely yours,
A. C. SWINBURNE.

Mr. Watts desires me to add that he will write to thank you for his copy of the *Masque* as soon as he is again able to write.

very imperfect fragment, wanting the title-page and other leaves, was preserved among the many Landor treasures in the possession of Robert Browning. In March, 1893, a fine and perfect copy, having upon its fly-leaf a presentation inscription in the handwriting of its Author, came to light, and Mr. Wise had the good fortune to secure it. For various reasons he did not carry out Swinburne's suggestion to reprint the little volume.

LETTER CXXXVII

To Edward Dowden

*The Pines,
Putney Hill,
S.W.
April 21st, 1893.*

DEAR MR. DOWDEN,
    Please convey my thanks to the Committee for their most courteous and gratifying reception of my little song. I need not, I hope, say that I entirely appreciate the force and the justice of the objection raised to the objectionable line. In fact since I sent it off, and especially all this morning, I have been cudgelling my brains for a tolerable substitute, and after more than one attempt have hit upon this, which in default of a better I think may pass muster:

> *Watch the ravens flock to feast,
> Dense as round a death-struck beast,
> Black as night is black.*[1]

[1] The lines as originally written ran:
> *Watch the ravens flock to feast,
> Dark as robe or creed of priest,
> Black as night is black.*

The song duly appeared in *The Nineteenth Century*, May, 1893, pp. 725-726. It was subsequently included in *Astrophel and Other Poems*, 1894, pp. 114-116. When published the discarded line underwent still further amendment, and now reads:
> *Dense as round some death-struck beast.*

Let me say that nothing could give me more pain than to know that I had given cause of offence to any Roman Catholic loyalist.

Indeed I cannot adequately express my admiration for the noble independence and conscientious dignity of the position they have taken up in face of the attitude assumed by such priests and bishops of their Church as those of whom—and whom alone—I was thinking when I wrote the words to which objection has naturally and rightly been taken.

The text of the song is already "booked" for the May number of *The Nineteenth Century*. I am of course much gratified to hear of the decision to ask Sir A. Sullivan to write music for it.

Ever sincerely yours,
A. C. SWINBURNE.

LETTER CXXXVIII

To Edward Dowden

The Pines,
Putney Hill,
S.W.
April 29th, 1893.

DEAR MR. DOWDEN,

Mr. Knowles is of course aware that my song *The Union* is to be set to music: but I think it would gratify him if you were to communicate with him on the subject.

So much for mere business, to begin with. Now let me thank you cordially for your letter of the 23rd, and assure you of the sincere sorrow and sympathy with which I received the intimation of your bereavement. I am looking forward with great interest to the perusal of your article in *The Fortnightly Review*.

What a noble and truthful saying was that of the Bishop of Derry![1] His name reminded me of an occasion—some thirty years ago—when the late D. G. Rossetti called my attention to the admirable qualities of his poetry.

Sincerely yours,
A. C. SWINBURNE.

LESSON CXXXIX

To Edmund Gosse

The Pines.
June 4th, [18]93.

MY DEAR GOSSE,
Thanks for your interesting article on Miss Rossetti. There is a misprint or mistake on

[1] William Alexander (1824-1911), who had been since 1867 Bishop of Derry, became in this year, 1893, Primate of All Ireland.

p. 212. Byron's Polidori[1] was, I have always understood, her mother's brother—not, as you say, uncle. And how came you to forget the graceful lines which commemorate her return from her one visit to Italy?

Have you read her commentary on *The Apocalypse*—between 500 and 600 closely printed pages? I HAVE—from the first line to the last—and yet I live!

Ever sincerely yours,
A. C. SWINBURNE.

LETTER CXL

To Clement K. Shorter

The Pines.
October 1st, 1893.

DEAR MR. SHORTER,

I am glad to hear of the service you are doing to Henry Kingsley's memory.[2] I cannot undertake to supply you with any "reminiscences," but I may suggest that you should reprint the fine account of *Eyre's Ride* from *Macmillan's Maga-*

---

[1] John William Polidori (1795-1821).
[2] An edition of the Collected Works of Henry Kingsley, in twelve volumes, was published under the editorship of Mr. Clement Shorter. *Eyre's Ride* was duly included, as suggested by Swinburne.

zine. I forget the date. It was, I think, in two parts or numbers.

Yours very truly,
A. C. SWINBURNE.

LETTER CXLI

To WILLIAM MORRIS

The Pines,
Putney Hill,
S.W.
January 23rd, 1894.

MY DEAR MORRIS,

Many thanks for your beautiful little book,[1] which I read through last night at a sitting with much interest and enjoyment. There never was such type as yours—one could read Longfellow or Tupper in such type.

Ever sincerely yours,
A. C. SWINBURNE.

[1] This was Morris's translation from old French, *King Florus and the Fair Jehane,* printed at the Kelmscott Press, 1893.

LETTER CXLII

To Edmund Gosse

*The Pines,
Putney Hill,
S.W.
January* 31st, [18]94.

MY DEAR GOSSE,
Many thanks for your admirable and scholarly book,[1] on which one might write a commentary as long as itself. Can praise of such work go higher? There are scores of things I should like to say—*e.g.* that I should want absolutely irrefragable proof before I could believe that the author of such second-hand and tenth-rate trash as *Albumazar* was the author of so exquisite and delightful a comic or allegoric poem as *Lingua*. I wish, when mentioning the play of *Swetman Arraigned,* you had quoted the magnificent couplet on Justice.

Your printer wants looking after—he has made pretty nonsense of a line quoted on page 132.

With kind regards to Mrs. Gosse and yourself,
Ever sincerely yours,
A. C. SWINBURNE.

[1] *The Jacobean Poets,* 1894.

LETTER CXLIII

To Edmund Gosse

The Pines,
Putney Hill,
S.W.
February 2nd, [18]94.

My dear Gosse,
When a printer presumes to forget that he is a machine, and has as much right to think for himself as an inkstand, he always does realise the records of the devil in a jointstool, malevolent furniture, chairs and tables under diabolical possession—preserved in such chronicles as *Satan's Invisible World Displayed,* and *Pandemonium, or the Devil's Cloister.* I condole with you as a fellow-sufferer.
Yours very sincerely,
A. C. Swinburne.

LETTER CXLIV

To Edmund Gosse

The Pines,
Putney Hill,
S.W.
February 12th, [18]94.

My dear Gosse,
   Your letter of the 8th has given me great pleasure. I am glad you like my dedication [1] of the book now in the printer's hands, and glad to know it recalls your own early regard for my own earlier poems: but more especially glad if any verses of my writing may help to disprove the foul tradition of jealousy as natural among workers in our own or any other form of art. Was not that always incomprehensible and incredible to you as a boy? It always was to me.

I have just treated myself to a copy of your delightful edition of Hazlitt's *Conversations with Northcote*. Though N. was not exactly a Coleridge or a Goethe, the book reminds one of their *Conversations* in its amazing seesaw of alternative sense and nonsense, brilliant truth and drivelling error. His *Fables* I remember as delightful to my boyhood. I once saw a very pretty set of the

[1] The dedication of *Astrophel* to William Morris.

illustrations, separate—proofs on India paper—dirt-cheap, which I have often regretted that I did not snap up.

Ever sincerely yours,
A. C. SWINBURNE.

P.S.—I re-open this envelope to ask a question which you must not take the trouble to answer till (if ever) you have nothing better to do. On p. 263 of your edition, Northcote rebukes Hazlitt for reporting—and misreporting—*his* report or account of "Sir Walter"—Scott. I have twice hunted thro' the book (which sorely needs an index—all such books do) and cannot verify the reference.

LETTER CXLV

To Thomas J. Wise

The Pines,
Putney Hill,
S.W.
March 10th, 1894.

Dear Mr. Wise,

Many thanks for the lovely case you have bestowed on my copy of Landor's *American Letters*. I could wish it had been *Count Julian*, but it is pleasant to have anything of his so beautifully and serviceably covered. Did you see a day or two since that a copy of the rarest of all his books, the *introuvable Simonidea,* was sold in the same lot with a copy of his earliest volume of poems? I wish I could have seen it.

I cannot honestly say that I am interested in knowing what has become of my own old scrawls, which I thought had long since been consigned to keeping of Vulcan. But I am glad to know that you have them, if you care to have them.[1]

Yours very sincerely,
A. C. SWINBURNE.
Mr. Watts desires me to add his kind regards.

LETTER CXLVI

To Edmund Gosse

*The Pines,
Putney Hill,
S.W.
June 29th,* [1894].

MY DEAR GOSSE,

Pray convey my sincere acknowledgments to the Committee,[2] together with the expression of my regret that I shall be far away from

---

[1] The Manuscripts of some of Swinburne's early poems which Mr. Wise had then just acquired.
[2] The American Committee for the placing of a bust of Keats in the parish church of Hampstead.

London on the day when the bust is to be unveiled. I need not, surely, say how gladly and how gratefully I hear of this American tribute to a great English poet. All Englishmen to whom poetry is not "an unknown quantity" must feel that no expression of loyal and fraternal sympathy could be more graceful, more precious, or more just.

    Yours very sincerely,
      A. C. SWINBURNE.

LETTER CXLVII

TO THEODORE WATTS-DUNTON

Chestal.
September 1st, 1894.

MY DEAR WALTER,

  I find I have been a fortnight in acknowledging your last letter with thanks for the pleasure it had given me.

I have been doing a good bit more of Heywood, and have now only six more plays to deal with out of twenty-six. Also I have read a good deal of Chaucer in the very serviceable new Oxford edition. How especially lovely is the *Parliament of Fowls!* I think he never wrote anything more winsome.

I wrote to Myers what I am sure you would

have allowed to be "a sweet thing in letters" in answer to a really nice one from him. We can discuss the question *in re* Sir Jackass when we meet.

After a thick shower of proofs [1] which ceased suddenly, I have had none for many days. They stopped at p. 208, in the middle of a sentence in the essay on Hugo's second series (*Alpes et Pyrénées*) of *Notes of Travel*. My article on the *first* series, *France et Belgique*—of which no proof has been sent!—as well as those on *Dieu* and *Toute la Lyre* (the latter divided, in two consecutive numbers), appeared, you know, in *The Fortnightly*. Any publisher on this God's earth but Chatto would have got them and sent the proofs without giving you or me the trouble to bid him to do so and be damned.

September 2nd.

Here comes, before I am up, your note with the enclosures which I return as desired, with the note from myself as ditto. The reference to the best books abrupt and egotistical, but you desired me to make it, and I did.

Do you know Randle (*sic*) Holme's *Academy of Armony*, 1688, and whether it is procurable at any moderate price? It is the sweetest book of

[1] Proofs of *Studies in Prose and Poetry*, 1894.

pure science I know. The chapters on botany, natural history,

> zo, ornith, entom, etym, ethn } ology kept us all in fits by the hour as

I read out excerpts yesterday to my mother and sisters. I came upon Shakespeare's odd and rare word "nook-shotten" (spelt "nuke") in a chapter on national coinages; it was used to describe "a cob of Ireland" ($= 4s.\ 8d.$). But the rare words are numberless. It should be thoroughly ransacked by the new lexicographers.

I have been to Berkeley Castle. The sight of that infernal oubliette actually gave me a bad night.

With best remembrances,
Ever your affec: minor,
A. C. SWINBURNE.

SWINBURNE'S LETTERS

LETTER CXLVIII

To William Morris

The Pines,
S.W.
July 24th, 1895.

My dear Morris,

Thanks once again for such a magnificent present as only you can make.[1] I have already been dipping again into the text of Jason with ever fresh admiration and delight.

Gratefully yours,
A. C. Swinburne.

LETTER CXLIX

To Clement K. Shorter

The Pines,
Putney Hill,
S.W.
March 4th, 1896.

Dear Mr. Shorter,

I am sorry that I must—with many thanks—decline the invitation of the Omar Khayyám Club. As to the immortal tent-maker him-

---

[1] The Kelmscott Press edition of *The Life and Death of Jason*.

self, I believe I may claim to be one of his earliest English admirers. It is upwards of thirty-six years since I was introduced to him by D. G. Rossetti, who had just been introduced himself, I believe, by Mr. Whitley Stokes. At that time the first and best edition of FitzGerald's wonderful version was being sold off at a penny a copy, having proved hopelessly unsaleable at the published price of one shilling. We invested, I should think, in hardly less than sixpenny-worth apiece, and on returning to the stall next day for more found that we had sent up the market to the sinfully extravagant sum of twopence, an imposition which evoked from Rossetti a fervent and impressive remonstrance. Not so very long afterwards, if I mistake not, the price of a copy was thirty shillings. It is the only edition worth having, as FitzGerald, like the ass of genius he was, cut out of later editions the crowning stanza which is the core or kernel of the whole. As to the greatness of the poem I can say no more than I have tried to say in print. I know none to be compared with it for power, pathos, and beauty, in the same line of thought and work, except possibly Ecclesiastes; and magnificent as that is, I can hardly think the author comparable to Omar either as philosopher or as poet.

Yours very truly,
A. C. SWINBURNE.

SWINBURNE'S LETTERS

LETTER CL

TO EDMUND GOSSE

*The Pines,
Putney Hill,
S.W.
July 12th,* 1896.

MY DEAR GOSSE,
Thanks for your note, and for the honour you did my verses [1] in reading them. Will you kindly convey my thanks also to Mr. Dillon (whose letter to you I return), for his very courteous word of recognition which you were good enough to send me?

The horrible hot weather, which invariably disables me, must be my excuse to you and to him for the tardiness of this acknowledgment.

Yours ever,
A. C. SWINBURNE.

[1] Written for the performance of Marlowe's *Dr. Faustus*. Swinburne had telegraphed "Delighted and honoured if you could read verses," which Mr. Gosse accordingly did.

LETTER CLI

To Clement K. Shorter

*The Pines,
Putney Hill,
S.W.
September 28th,* 1896.

DEAR MR. SHORTER,
  A thousand thanks for your most handsome and valued present.[1] How full of interest it is to me at the very first glance I need not try to say. You do me too much honour by what you say of my tribute to those two immortal sisters. Mr. Watts-Dunton will be delighted to receive a copy of the book.

Perhaps it may be indiscreet of me to tell you that Lord Houghton once assured me that Bramwell Brontë's story about his mistress as related by Mrs. Gaskell was perfectly true. But "Dicky Milnes," as Tennyson and I suppose other contemporary friends used to call him, was not exactly a final or conclusive authority on such a matter—or, I should say, on any matter of fact. He was a good-natured old fellow, but when made into a peer his title might have been "Baron Tattle, of Scandal." However, I should incline to think he

[1] Mr. Shorter's *Charlotte Brontë and her Circle.* 8vo, 1896.

spoke truth on this occasion. He could hardly have ventured to say of an innocent lady living in his own county that her character was notorious.[1]

Yours sincerely and gratefully,
A. C. SWINBURNE.

LETTER CLII

TO CLEMENT K. SHORTER

*The Pines,
Putney Hill,
S.W.
October 19th, 1896.*

DEAR MR. SHORTER,

I have to thank you again for a most acceptable gift [2]—but I know not how we are to thank Mr. Nicholls for his truly generous surrender of personal inclination! Mr. Watts-Dunton asks me to join his thanks to mine, and to say how fully he shares my interest in this delightful and valuable book.

Lest I should forget to say it at all, let me begin by saying that while I by no means disagree on the whole with what you say about Mme. Darme-

---

[1] Lord Houghton may not have been unjust in saying that the lady's character was "notorious," but he was wrong in his assumption that Bramwell Brontë was her victim.—[*Note by Mr. Shorter.*]

[2] Mr. Shorter's *Charlotte Brontë and her Circle.* 8vo, 1896.

steter's book,[1] I think you have forgotten that the one new thing she had to tell us—how Emily saved her wretched brother from being burnt in his bed—is the most important thing we know about that wonderful poetess and heroine. Of course there is far too much in the book about him: but that one anecdote atones for all.[2] Is it not possible to recover his portrait of her?[3] Martha Brown must surely have treasured it. I would give anything in reason to see what she was like. Charlotte's bad eyesight must must have misled her when she fancied a likeness between her sister and G. H. Lewes. I only met him once, but I remember not only that he was the ugliest of human beings I ever saw except perhaps his consort George Eliot, but that it was not such a mean and vulgar ugliness as suggested nothing but the idea of a smart, pert, impudent counter-jumper. I no more believe in that likeness than I would believe that Homer or Sappho or Shakespeare or Vittoria Colonna could have been like that hideous smirking scribbler. And all the more do I wish to see what she *was* like. The letter printed at p. 47 would suffice of

[1] *Life of Emily Brontë,* by Mary F. Robinson, now Madame Duclaux.
[2] The anecdote is empty gossip, quite without verification. But I was unjust to Miss Robinson's book all the same.—[*Note by Mr. Shorter.*]
[3] It is now in the National Portrait Gallery.

itself to make your book most valuable to all readers fit to read it.

> Yours very gratefully,
> A. C. SWINBURNE.

LETTER CLIII

To Thomas J. Wise

> *The Pines,*
> *Putney Hill,*
> *S.W.*
> *November 2nd,* 1896.

DEAR MR. WISE,

I am really overwhelmed by the magnificence of your generosity. No gift could be more precious to me, and no one could prize it more than I.[1] What an exquisite hand! Finer than the finest diamond type. As to the matter of the letter, you know what I think. I need not tell you how the admirable vignette of the sea—worthy of Turner, had he been a writer—appeals to my sympathy. I should rather have expected it from Emily than from Charlotte. I suppose you have

[1] In 1896 Mr. Wise purchased from the Rev. Arthur Bell Nichols, husband of Charlotte Brontë, a number of the early Manuscripts of the Brontë children, written in their well-known microscopic hand. The collection also included some of Charlotte's letters. Knowing Swinburne's keen interest in all that concerned the Brontë family, Mr. Wise gave a small selection of these Manuscripts to him.

no evidence as to the sea's influence over the younger sister. Perhaps her passion for the moors—which I, as a Borderer, have always thought the next best thing to the sea—absorbed and superseded all other affections of the kind. Mr. Watts-Dunton, who thoroughly sympathizes with my appreciation of the treasure which I owe to your kindness, sends his most cordial regards to accompany those of

   Yours very gratefully,
     A. C. SWINBURNE.

LETTER CLIV

To SIDNEY C. COCKERELL

The Pines.
January 8th, 1897.

DEAR MR. COCKERELL,

Many thanks for your beautiful and valuable gift.[1] I can imagine Morris reading out these sonorous couplets. I have written several hymns in the same language—if mediæval dog-Latin or priest-Latin may be called a language—

---

[1] *Laudis beatae Mariae virginis,* edited by S. C. Cockerell, and printed at the Kelmscott Press from a 13th century Psalter in Morris's library. The "slip" states that a printed copy of the same verses exists (Tegernsæ, 1579) in which the authorship is ascribed to Stephen Langton.—[S. C. C.]

but not in this striking and effective metre—the slip at the end is most interesting.

> Yours very sincerely,
> A. C. SWINBURNE.

LETTER CLV

To SIDNEY C. COCKERELL

> [*Putney.*]
> *January 20th,* 1897.

DEAR MR. COCKERELL,
    A thousand thanks for your beautiful and precious gift.[1] Why did not Morris take up and finish Froissart earlier—instead of the less appropriate work (Shelley, for one instance) on which the Kelmscott Press was occasionally wasted?

> Very gratefully yours,
> A. C. SWINBURNE.

[1] Two folio leaves of the projected Kelmscott *Froissart* printed on vellum after Morris's death had caused the abandonment of the work.—[S. C. C.]

LETTER CLVI

TO SIR SIDNEY LEE

June 24th, 1897.

MY DEAR SIR,
 I have read your article on Shakespeare with great interest, and am no less grateful for the gift of it than gratified by what you say of my Study.
 With many thanks,
  Yours very truly,
   A. C. SWINBURNE.

LETTER CLVII

TO THOMAS HARDY

The Pines,
Putney Hill,
S.W.
December 26th, 1898.

DEAR MR. HARDY,
 Many and cordial thanks for your delightful volume [1] which I received a few days ago. Both the poems and the illustrations have now been studied by others as well as by me with uni-

[1] *Wessex Poems,* 1898.

versal admiration and keen interest. It would be almost impertinent to specify my special favourites, but perhaps I may take leave to say that I admire none more than the frontispiece so happily chosen and the poem it illustrates, the splendid illustrations to pages 75, 78, 113 and the poems "In a Wood," "The Fire at Tranter Sweatley's," "Her Death and After," "The Slow Nature," "The Dance at the Phœnix," and here I must draw bridle, or I shall be citing more than half the contents.

Yours very gratefully,
A. C. SWINBURNE.

LETTER CLVIII

To EDMUND GOSSE

The Pines.
March 18th, [18]99.

MY DEAR GOSSE,
Thanks for the trouble you have kindly taken in the elucidation of *Locrine*. What you are good enough to say about the effect of the various arrangements in rhyme is all the more gratifying because it was said when the play was published that even if it ever could be put on the stage they would surely drive any audience to distraction! (There is something irregularly like

them in Greene's *Selimus,* as well as in Lord Brooke's toughest of dramatic indigestibles.)

I did not mean to represent Locrine as at all melancholy or given to mysticism, though harassed and worried at times by his false position in a double life, but naturally of a turn of mind as joyous and sunny as Guendolen's is gloomy and fiery; nor Estrild as a "meek slave," but a loving and grateful morganatic wife, sometimes a little dissatisfied with her lot, but never going further than a gentle and uncomplaining hint to that effect. What you say of Guendolen hits off exactly what I meant.

I do not remember having invented anything about Albanact (is it he whom you mean by "the heroic son of Brutus"?), but the envious princelet Camber I thought an original figure.

Watts-Dunton has been, I am sorry to say, seriously ill, and unable to write any letters. He is much better now, but does not go out yet.

Very sincerely yours,
A. C. SWINBURNE.

LETTER CLIX

To Edward Henry Blakeney

*The Pines,
Putney Hill,
S.W.
October* 12*th*, 1899.

Dear Sir,
Thanks for your note and the enclosed verses, which to some extent remind me of Matthew Arnold; not as an imitation of his style, but as an instance of natural sympathy in emotion and expression.

I still think the selected chorus [1] rather dismal for boys, and I fancy even the few who may be at all inclined towards poetry would have preferred the lyric narrative in *The Armada* of the flight of the routed enemy from the Channel northward, and south again to Ireland—with the sort of hymn that follows in praise of England, and exultation over the ruin and disgrace of her enemies.

It is too long to learn off by heart, but I think boys who do not simply abhor verse would relish

[1] Mr. Blakeney had written to Swinburne asking leave to include in a proposed book of verse repetition for schools one or two of his pieces, in particular the great chorus in *Atalanta,* "Before the beginning of years."

the movement and impulse of it—if not the militant patriotism which ought to be more to their taste than the classic pessimism of *Atalanta*.
Yours sincerely,
A. C. SWINBURNE.

LETTER CLX

TO CLEMENT K. SHORTER

The Pines.
February 2nd, 1900.

DEAR MR. SHORTER,
Thanks for *The Sphere,* which strikes me as generally admirable, and for your kindness in putting me on the free list, which but for an accident or oversight would of course have been acknowledged before this. The portrait of Ruskin is beyond all praise, and that of Dr. Martineau is almost as fine and lifelike. I am told that others are not less good, but it is only of these two that I can judge from personal recollection.
Yours very truly,
A. C. SWINBURNE.

LETTER CLXI

TO SIR SIDNEY LEE

The Pines.
June 20th, [1900].

DEAR MR. LEE,
I fear I must have forgotten that my little article on Nabbes was pre-engaged.[1] If Mr. Watts-Dunton and I could at some future time manage a visit to the library at Bridgewater House, we should of course be gratified, and interested, to avail ourselves of the privilege.
Yours sincerely,
A. C. SWINBURNE.

LETTER CLXII

TO EDMUND GOSSE

The Pines.
July 12th, [1900].

MY DEAR GOSSE,
The man who would undertake to write the very shortest article on Richard Burton's life

---

[1] Swinburne's essay on Nabbes was intended to form a chapter in the Second Series of *The Age of Shakespeare.* But this volume, though long projected, is only now in the press, and the essay was ultimately printed alone under the title, *Thomas Nabbes. A Critical Monograph. London: Printed for Private Circulation,* 1914.

and work should be far better equipped for a rather arduous task than I. I could only bear my witness, from personal experience, that no kindlier man, no more loyal friend, ever lived—and that no more delightful companion can be imagined, either in his most serious or his most humorous moods.

Yours sincerely,
A. C. SWINBURNE.

LETTER CLXIII
To SIDNEY C. COCKERELL

The Pines.
November 22nd, [1900].

DEAR MR. COCKERELL,
Your very kind note of the 8th was mislaid by some accident and I have only just found and opened it. I have now read *A Dream of John Ball,* and think it a singularly beautiful piece of writing. I prefer above all else that I have read of W. M.'s prose work—there is a good deal that I have not, and probably never shall—*The Well at the World's End.*
I am

Yours gratefully,
A. C. SWINBURNE.

[Swinburne told me on January 7th, 1897, that he read *The Well at the World's End* out of doors at High Oaks.—S.C.C.]

LETTER CLXIV

TO WILLIAM SHARP

*The Pines,
Putney Hill,
London,
S.W.
October 6th,* 1901.

DEAR MR. SHARP,

Many thanks for the early copy [1] you have had the kindness to send on to me. I am pleased to find the *Nympholept* in a leading place, as I think it one of the best and most representative things I ever did. I should have preferred on all accounts that *In the Bay* had filled the place you have allotted to *Ave atque Vale,* a poem to which you are altogether too kind in my opinion, as others have been before you. I never had really much in common with Baudelaire, though I retain all my early admiration for his genius at its best. I wish there were fewer of such very juvenile crudities as you have selected from my first volume of Poems: it is trying to find such boyish attempts as *The Sundew, Aholibah, Madonna Mia,* etc., offered as examples of the work of a man who has written so many volumes since in which there is nothing that is not at least better and riper than

[1] Of the Tauchnitz volume of *Selections* from Swinburne's Poems, edited by William Sharp.

they. I wish too that *Mater Triumphalis* had not been separated from its fellow poem—a much fitter piece of work to stand by itself. On the other hand I am very cordially obliged to you for giving the detached extract from *Anactoria*. I should greatly have preferred that extracts only should have been given from *Atalanta in Calydon,* which sorely needs compression in the earlier parts. *Erechtheus,* which would have taken up so much less space, would also, I venture to think, have been a better and a fairer example of the author's works. Mr. Watts-Dunton's objection to the book is the omission of *Super Flumina Babylonis*. I too am much surprised to find it excluded from a selection which includes so much that might well be spared —nay, would be better away. I would like to have seen one of what I call my topographical poems in full. The tiny scrap from *Loch Torridon* was hardly worth giving by itself. I do not understand what you find obscure or melancholy in *The Garden of Cymodoce*. It was written principally to express my constant delight in the recollection of Sark.

I hope you will not think anything in this note captious or ungracious. Candour always seems to be the best expression possible of gratitude or goodwill.

Ever sincerely yours,
A. C. SWINBURNE.

LETTER CLXV

TO CLEMENT K. SHORTER

> The Pines,
> Putney Hill,
> S.W.
> *April* 11th, 1902.

DEAR MR. SHORTER,

Many thanks for a very charming little volume.[1] I was very much taken with *The Beggar Maid* when I read it in *Longman's Magazine*. The first poem in the book is very striking: and the story of *The Dean of Santiago* is a curious and interesting version of the legend or moral so wonderfully retold and reconveyed in Browning's *Pietro of Abano*. I should have liked to know more of *The Man who Trod on Sleeping Grass*. It is curiously like and unlike a North-English or South-Scottish fairy superstition. Of all fairy poems in the world the loveliest and eeriest is the mediæval North Country romance of Orfeo and Heurodis—Orpheus, King of Winchester (a city formerly known by the name of Thrace, as the poet is careful to explain), and Queen Eurydice his wife, who was stolen away by the fairies, but

[1] *The Woman who went to Hell, and Other Ballads and Lyrics*. By Dora Sigerson, *i.e.* Mrs. Clement Shorter. London. 8vo, 1902.

finally restored to the arms of H. M. of Winchester. The description of fairyland is simply one of the most exquisitely imaginative and beautiful things in the language. The only edition I know is so rare that I presume you have not read it: if you have, I apologise, and feel sure that you both agree with me. I read it aloud not long since to my sisters, and they did most thoroughly.

I must add that Mr. Watts-Dunton is as warm an admirer of *The Beggar Maid* as I am.

Yours very sincerely,
A. C. SWINBURNE.

LETTER CLXVI

To the Right Hon. D. H. Madden

The Pines,
Putney Hill,
S.W.
August 10th, 1902.

DEAR SIR,

I am greatly obliged by the gift of your delightful book.[1]

Some years since I spent a very pleasant time at Dursley and made acquaintance with much of the country east and west, so that I can the better appreciate the truth and charm of your references to

---

[1] *The Diary of Master William Silence.*

that beautiful and unspoilt neighbourhood and its associations with the work of the greatest among all men of all time.

I am sincerely glad to know that my article on Dickens has given you pleasure—and I remain
Very sincerely yours,
A. C. SWINBURNE.

LETTER CLXVII

To SIDNEY C. COCKERELL

The Pines,
11 *Putney Hill,*
S.W.
[*August* 5th, 1903.]

DEAR MR. COCKERELL,

I am equally interested and delighted to hear what you tell me. I trust you will make it public. The appreciation of so great a man as Tolstoy—so glorious a genius and so glorious a personality—does what no other living man's could do—it adds a crowning ray of glory to the fame of Dickens. Above all, what a superb and crushing reply to the vulgar insults of such malignant boobies and poetasters as G. H. Lewes & Co. (too numerous a Co!) is the witness of such a man as this—such a man of men—to the lifetime reality of his characters and their capacity to make themselves our "personal friends!"

SWINBURNE'S LETTERS

I thank you for having given me a very keen pleasure and a very deep satisfaction. After all, like will to like—genius will find out genius, and goodness will recognise goodness.

Yours gratefully,
A. C. SWINBURNE.

[I visited Tolstoy in July, 1903, and reported to Swinburne that he had said of Dickens "All his characters are my personal friends—I am constantly comparing them with living persons, and living persons with them, and what a spirit there was in all he wrote."—S.C.C.]

LETTER CLXVIII

To Thomas Hardy

The Pines,
Putney Hill.
January 23rd, [1904].

Dear Mr. Hardy,

Had I been better able to write while still confined to my room I should have thanked you earlier for your gift of *The Dynasts*. It has a double interest for me, whose father served as a midshipman under Collingwood,[1] and knew Lady Hester Stanhope in her later days when an Eastern princess and prophetess. She was, I believe, very civil and pleasant to him, and I always as a boy

---

[1] This appears to have been a misapprehension on Algernon Swinburne's part.

thought what fun it must have been as an experience. But between him and his old captain there was a strong mutual regard and affectionate esteem—well proved on both sides—of much more serious interest and import. By the way, I know the old story of "tapping the Admiral," but surely it was not Nelson, was it?[1]

I never read any dialogue of yours that gave me more delight than the fifth scene of the second act, nor any verse of yours that I more admired than the noble song which closes the fifth act. But if I may say it without offence—I trust you do not mean to give over your great work in creative romance even for the field of epic or historic drama.

Very sincerely yours,
A. C. SWINBURNE.

LETTER CLXIX

To JOHN H. INGRAM

The Pines,
Putney Hill,
S.W.
January 23rd, 1904.

DEAR MR. INGRAM,
    Nothing could give me more pleasure than to hear of your successful good work on behalf

[1] [I have always heard it related of Nelson.—T. H.]

of the first great English poet. Any tribute to his memory cannot but afford me pleasure. Those that I have paid are so numerous, both in verse and prose, that I can hardly remember them all; but the more of them you do me the honour to cite the more gratified I shall naturally be. I think it is in the article on the rather poor old play of *King Edward III.* appended to my *Study of Shakespeare* that I have done homage to the great passage in *Tamburlaine* on the ideal of poetry and poets as the greatest thing ever written, I might safely have added "that ever will be written," on the subject. In the second series of *Poems and Ballads* the greater part of the second poem (*In the Bay*) is addressed to Marlowe, and in part to Shelley as his successor (stanzas 8 to 40).

In the volume *Astrophel and Other Poems,* (pages 121–2) there are four quatrains which of course are not inscribed on the memorial actually raised to his memory.[1] This is all I can now remember—and more than enough to have deserved the ridicule and invective of "verminous fellows" who think and write after their kind.

I must allow myself to add that I hope you will not overdo the good work of rehabilitation. Whatever rests only on Puritan authority I should of course assume to be a lie—not a probable lie but

[1] An obscure, and wholly inadequate, memorial to Marlowe at Canterbury, the place of his birth—see *ante,* pp. 205-206.

an indisputable lie. But I shall never believe that he was a Keble or a Wordsworth—or that he had not more kinship with Burns and Villon than with Milton (who learnt of him) or with Tennyson (who learnt of Milton).

The cutting you enclose mentions that your work "will be illustrated by portraits, etc." I fear it must be surely too much to hope that you can have discovered any authentic portrait—however rough—of Him? I would rather see that than any other man's likeness—and next to it Webster's—and next to that, Tourneur's (or Turner's).

Ever sincerely yours,
A. C. SWINBURNE.

LETTER CLXX

To JOHN H. INGRAM

The Pines,
Putney Hill,
S.W.
June 30th, 1904.

DEAR MR. INGRAM,
I must beg you to excuse an apparently inexcusable but really involuntary and purely accidental delay in acknowledging your valuable present [1] and the accompanying letter. Your beau-

[1] A copy of *Christopher Marlowe and his Associates,* by John H. Ingram, London, 1904.

tiful volume, of such great interest to all students of poetry, is of peculiar interest to me, who have always recognized in Marlowe the greatest of our poets before Shakespeare—if not indeed, properly speaking, our first absolutely great poet; the first to deserve the highest epithet which can be assigned to any—sublime.

By your noble vindication of his deathless memory you have done a great and memorable service, not to his name alone, but to the nation and the race of which that name is one among the crowning glories.

I most cordially congratulate and thank you.
Yours most truly,
A. C. SWINBURNE.

LETTER CLXXI

To SIDNEY C. COCKERELL

The Pines,
11 *Putney Hill,*
S.W.
October, [190]4.

DEAR MR. COCKERELL,
I hope you have not thought me the most ungracious of ingrates for not acknowledging your too generous present by return of post. I had not anything of my own to send till to-day, as I never keep my manuscripts, but always make them

over to a friend, and I did not like to write a letter of mere thanks without any enclosure such as you might care to accept. The poem of which I am now able to send you the manuscript is rather a favourite of mine from past associations connected with the garden described in it.[1]

    Yours sincerely,
      A. C. SWINBURNE.

LETTER CLXXII

To SIDNEY C. COCKERELL

The Pines,
April 30, [190]5.

DEAR MR. COCKERELL,
  I am somewhat late in acknowledging with most cordial thanks your generous gift of what I am determined to believe a good and true as well as a noble and beautiful likeness of my hero.[2]

    Yours gratefully,
      A. C. SWINBURNE.

---

[1] [On September 29 I dined with Swinburne and Watts-Dunton and showed them an Ovid containing Ben Jonson's signature. Swinburne was so deeply interested in it, that I decided the next day to send it to him, and wrote that if he did not care to accept it without making some return I should be very pleased to have a scrap of his manuscript. He very generously sent me, with the above letter, the manuscript of *Astrophel*.—S. C. C.]

[2] [A photograph of the picture by an unknown artist in the Museo Civico at Venice, formerly regarded as a portrait of Cæsar Borgia.—S. C. C.]

LETTER CLXXIII

To Sidney C. Cockerell

*The Pines,
Putney Hill,
S.W.*
January 11th, 1906.

Dear Mr. Cockerell,
 I hardly know which to thank first, yourself or Lord Lovelace. I remember meeting him very well, and am sincerely glad to know that he has retained so kindly a memory of me. Pray give him my cordial thanks for the really splendid present which I await with very great interest. I know what a favour it is even to be allowed a sight of the book. It must be of quite unique interest.

I need not say how much both Watts-Dunton and myself would enjoy a sight of your San Graal MS. I wish my uncle Ashburnham, whose collection is now scattered to the winds, were alive to see it—as well as Burne Jones and Morris.

Any evening that would suit your convenience would naturally suit ours, if you will let us know beforehand.

 Yours with sincere gratitude,
 A. C. Swinburne.

[The first part of the above letter refers to Lord Lovelace's *Astarte,* a copy of which he gave to Swinburne at my suggestion. The second to a magnificent thirteenth-century MS. of *Lancelot du Lac,* which happened to have come from Lord Ashburnham's collection.

Extract from my diary, January 16th, 1906: "Went to the Pines and talked with Swinburne and Watts-Dunton about Lord Lovelace's *Astarte.* Swinburne very scornful of Lady Byron for confiding in Mrs. Beecher Stowe, but not much interested in Byron, his whole admiration being given to Coleridge, Shelley and Keats."—S. C. C.]

LETTER CLXXIV

To the Earl Curzon of Kedleston

The Pines,
Putney Hill,
S.W.
May 3rd, 1907.

Dear Lord Curzon,

I am much honoured and gratified by the far too complimentary terms in which you offer me a distinction [1] which I must decline to accept. But I am not the less sensible of your courtesy or the less hopeful that you will not regard me as ungrateful for it.

I am,
Yours very truly,
A. C. Swinburne.

[1] An honorary degree at Oxford.

LETTER CLXXV

To Lady Ritchie

The Pines.
January 22nd, '08.

DEAR LADY RITCHIE,
Many thanks for sending me Miss Coleridge's poems.[1] They are full of beauty and charm—charm which does not belong to all beautiful writing and delicate execution. It is high praise for me to say that they often remind me of Mrs. Shorter's (born Dora Sigerson) which I hope you know and admire as I do.

I do congratulate you cordially on being a grandmother. To have a baby at hand or within reach is to belong to "the kingdom of heaven" yourself. I met this morning on my daily walk a fair friend not yet well stricken in months, who beamed and chuckled inarticulately (being still by necessity an inarticulate poet) at sight of me from the depth of her pushwainling. (I hope you never use the barbaric word perambulator?) Don't you like the late Rev. W. Barnes much better as a Lexicographer (though I fear Miss Pinkerton might

[1] Mary Elizabeth Coleridge (1861-1907), whose *Collected Poems* were published, by Sir Henry Newbolt, after her death in 1907.

have demurred to his claims on that score) than as a poet? The happy term "pushwainling" for a baby's coach of state, is what makes him immortal in my eyes.

Sir Theodore Watts-Dunton belongs to the same order of creation as Mrs. Harris, but Mr. T. W.-D. is none the less grateful for your so kindly misplaced congratulations.

Ever sincerely and cordially yours,
A. C. SWINBURNE.

LETTER CLXXVI

To A. H. BULLEN

The Pines,
11 Putney Hill,
S.W.
October 11th, 1908.

DEAR SIR,
I had already read with great pleasure your admirable article on my book, and am delighted to know that it is you whom I have to thank for it, as for so much else. Mr. Watts-Dunton wishes me to tell you how much delight he takes in your priceless collection of old plays, to which (thanks to your generosity) I have had the pleasure of introducing him.

Ever gratefully yours,
A. C. SWINBURNE.

LETTER CLXXVII

To A. H. Bullen

The Pines,
11 Putney Hill,
S.W.
January 11th, 1909.

My dear Sir,
　　　　　I am sorry I could not (or anyhow did not) manage to answer your note of the 4th till this evening—having a good many calls on my time, besides being an "idle old man" like King Lear.

I should be glad to do anything which you would take as a personal compliment, but I could not undertake the task proposed. The best possible introduction to the *Sonnets* was many years ago prefixed by François Victor Hugo to his matchless and marvellous translation of them. You could not possibly, in my opinion, do better than get some competent scholar to send you by way of preface a close and careful version of it.

With all reciprocated good wishes for the New Year.

　　　　　　Ever sincerely yours,
　　　　　　　A. C. Swinburne.

INDEX

Academy, The, i, 213, 249, 260; ii, 67, 69, 97
Academy of Armony, by R. Holme, ii, 241
AESCHYLUS, *Erechtheus* modelled after style of, i, 223-4
AINGER, A., ii, 115, 120
ALACOQUE, Marie, i, 235
ALBANY, Duke of, Swinburne's account of, i, 270-1
Albigenses, The, by A. C. Swinburne, i, 5
Alcilia: Philoparthen's Loving Pollie, ii, 54
Alcyone, by E. Gosse, ii, 40, 44
Aline et Valcour, i, 293
ALISON, Dr., i, 54
All's Lost by Lust, by W. Rowley, ii, 23
American Letters, by W. S. Landor, ii, 238
Anactoria, i, 51, 235
APPLETON, Dr., i, 260
L'Après-Midi d'un Faune, by S. Mallarmé, i, 252
Arden of Ferversham, by G. Lillo, ii, 149, 150, 164
Armada, The, by A. C. Swinburne, ii, 199, 202, 255
ARNOLD, Matthew, i, 289; ii, 41, 80, 255
ASHBURNHAM, Charlotte, Countess of, death of, i, 15
L'Assommoir, by Emile Zola, ii, 12, 32
Astarte, by Lord Lovelace, ii, 271
Astrophel and Other Poems, by A. C. Swinburne, ii, 213, 230, 237, 266, 269
Atalanta in Calydon, by A. C. Swinburne, correspondence *re* printing of, i, 23

Atalanta in Calydon, date of composition, i, 186
—— Lord Houghton's article on, Swinburne's appreciation, i, 286
—— Maurice's description of, Swinburne quotes, i, 39
—— payment for, i, 192
—— Swinburne's account of writing, i, 23-4
—— references, i, 46, 286; ii, 256
Atheist's Tragedy, The, by Cyril Tourneur, i, 109; ii, 17
Athenæum, The, ERECHTHEUS reviewed in, i, 224, 227; *re* publication of poems and prose in, i, 91-3, 222, 227; ii, 2, 3, 7, 9
—— references, i, 222, 308; ii, 2, 4, 28, 132, 173, 176, 213
Athens: an Ode, by A. C. Swinburne, ii, 85, 94, 112
Aurora Leigh, by E. B. Browning, i, 1

Ballad of Bulgarie, by A. C. Swinburne, i, 258, 262, 265; ii, 56
Ballad of Dreamland, The, by A. C. Swinburne, ii, 23
BARNES, Rev. W., ii, 272
Battle of Evesham, MS. by B. Barnes, ii, 107, 109, 138
BAUDELAIRE, i, 89, 128, 131, 169, 204-5, 207, 246, 289; ii, 259
Beauchamp's Career, by G. Meredith, Swinburne's criticism of, i, 239
BEAUMONT AND FLETCHER, Swinburne's article on, for *Encyclopædia Britannica*, i, 304
Before Sunset, by A. C. Swinburne, i, 93
BEHN, Mrs. Aphra, ii, 84
BENDYSHE, Mr., i, 293
Biographia Dramatica, ii, 15, 173

INDEX

BIRD, Miss A., letter to, ii, 157
BLAKE, William, i, 166, 235, 245, 253, 290–1
Blake, by A. C. Swinburne, i, 46, 51 245, 253, 281, 284, 290
BLAKENEY, Mr. Edward Henry, letter to, ii, 255–6
BLIND, Karl, i, 267, 274; ii, 78
BOLINGBROKE, Lord, ii, 168
BONAPARTE-WYSE, William, i, 203
BONCHURCH, funeral of Swinburne's father at, ii, 1, 2
Bonshommes, by Léon Cladel, ii, 51
BORGIA, Lucrezia, i, 12
Bothwell, i, 83, 97, 113, 134, 148–9, 295, 296
BOYLE, Robert, ii, 128
BRANDES, Dr. Georg, i, 166
BRETON, Nicholas, ii, 54
BREWER, A., ii, 184
BRONTË, P. B., ii, 247
BRONTË, Charlotte, Swinburne's Essay on, ii, 13, 172
Brontë, Life of Emily, by Mary F. Robinson, ii, 248
BROUGHTON, Lord, i, 57; ii, 167
BROWN, Ford Madox, i, 27, 95; ii, 24
BROWNING, Robert, i, 12, 34, 87, 124, 173, 181, 222, 234, 240, 306; ii, 32, 33, 38, 39, 43, 55, 80, 131, 209, 217
BUCHANAN, Robert, i, 94, 140, 150–1; ii, 20
BULLEIN, W., ii, 197–9
BULLEN, Mr. A. H., letters to, ii, 106–10, 119–22, 127–30, 137–8, 144–5, 147–53, 156–7, 158–65, 180–5, 186–7, 196–200, 201–4, 207–9, 210–13, 273, 274
BULLEN, Mr. A. H., Old English Plays edited by, ii, 106
BURDEN, Edith (Mrs. William Morris), i, 2, 5
BURNE-JONES, Sir E., i, 48, 90
——, letter to, ii, 216–19, 270
BURNS, Robert, i, 211
BURROUGHS, Mr., ii, 139
BURTON, Sir R. F., letters to, i, 48–51

BURTON, Sir R. F., references, i, 30, 287; ii, 25
BURTON, Mrs., i, 51, 57, 296; ii, 61
BYRON, committee for monument to, Swinburne's attitude towards, i, 138, 250
——, references, ii, 140, 167, 180
Byron, by A. C. Swinburne, i, 34, 37, 38, 57; ii, 80
Byron's Tragedy, by G. Chapman, i, 147

CADOL, V. E., i, 299
Cæsar Borgia, by Nathaniel Lee, ii, 209
CAINE, HALL, ii, 103
CAMPBELL, Thomas, i, 211
CAMPION, ii, 207
Captain Underwit, anonymous play, ii, 127
CARLYLE, Thomas, i, 25, 226; ii, 33, 55, 103, 117, 122, 148
Cassell's Magazine, Swinburne's translation of Victor Hugo's "Les Enfants Pauvres" in, i, 69
CATULLUS, i, 172
CENTLIVRE, Mrs., ii, 23
Century of Roundels, A, by A. C. Swinburne, ii, 132
CHAPMAN, G., i, 120, 143–4, 146–8, 151, 157–66, 173–4, 299, ii, 110, 159.
CHAPMAN & HALL, publishing transactions with, i, 100, 112
Characteristics of English poets from Chaucer to Shirley, by W. Minto, i, 166
CHARLEMONTE, Lord, i, 284
Charlotte Brontë and her Circle, by C. K. Shorter, ii, 247
CHARTRES, Vidame de, ii, 10–11
Chastelard, by A. C. Swinburne, i, 9, 34–5, 46; ii, 77, 188, 190
CHATTO, Mr., i, 162, 163, 175, 197, 202, 213; ii, 23, 241
CHAUCER, i, 242; ii, 240
Childe Roland, by R. Browning, i, 10
Child's Garden of Verses, by R. L. Stevenson, ii, 155

INDEX

Choice of Valentines, The, by Nash, ii, 221
Christabel and the Lyrical and Imaginative Poems of S. T. Coleridge, arranged and introduced by A. C. Swinburne, i, 61
Christian turned Turk, A, by Robert Daborne, ii, 107
Christmas Carol, A, by A. C. Swinburne, ii, 142
CLADEL, Léon, ii, 51
Cleopatra, by A. C. Swinburne, ii, 187, 189, 194
COCKERELL, Mr. Sidney C., letters to, ii, 250, 251, 258, 263, 268, 269, 270
COLERIDGE, M. E., ii, 272
COLERIDGE, S. T., Poems of, edited by A. C. Swinburne, i, 61
—— rhyme of, Swinburne's comments on, i, 68
Collection of Old English Plays, A, edited by A. H. Bullen, ii, 106–10, 119–20, 127–30, 137–8
Collette, Stanzas to Mr., ii, 34, 36
COLLINGWOOD, Admiral, ii, 264
COLLINS, John Churton, ii, 18, 128, 176
—— letters to, i, 109–12, 196–7, 248–50, 257–8; ii, 18–19, 93–4, 98, 115–19, 124–5, 168–9
COLLINS, William, Poems of, Swinburne's proposal to edit, ii, 42, 47
COLVIN, Sir Sidney, Letters to, i, 97–100; ii, 86, 93
Commemoration Ode, by J. R. Lowell, i, 200
Complaint of Mona Lisa, The, by A. C. Swinburne, i, 67; ii, 9
Comus, by John Milton, ii, 115
CONGREVE, William, Swinburne's article on, i, 256
Contemplations, Les, by Victor Hugo, ii, 76
CONWAY, Moncure, i, 47, 192
Cornhill Magazine, ii, 187, 188
CORNISH, F. W., letter to, ii, 213–4

CORNWALL, Barry. *See* Procter, B. W.
Coronation, The, by W. S. Landor, ii, 58
Costlie Whore, The, ii, 107, 137, 145, 150
Count Julian, by W. S. Landor, i, 125
Court of Love, The, by A. C. Swinburne, ii, 3, 9
CRUIKSHANK, circumstances of, reference, i, 37
CURZON OF KEDLESTON, Earl, letter to, ii, 271
Cynthia's Revels, by Ben Jonson, ii, 108
Cynthia's Revenge, anonymous play (1613), ii, 107, 108, 197

Daily News, i, 178
DANTE, i, 229
DAVENPORT, Robert, i, 255; ii, 145, 149, 159, 161, 196, 210
DAY, J., ii, 119
Dead Love, by A. C. Swinburne, ii, 195
Death of Anne Boleyn, The, by W. S. Landor, ii, 58
Death of Marlowe, The, by R. H. Horne, ii, 147
Defence of Guenevere, by W. Morris, i, 1–2, 6
DEKKER, Thomas, i, 153; ii, 148, 159, 160
Devil's Charter, The, by Barnabe Barnes (1607), ii, 109
Diary of Master William Silence, The, by D. H. Madden, ii, 263
DICKENS, Charles, i, 113; ii, 263-4
DIDEROT, i, 214, 240, 306–7
DIERX, Léon, i, 244
DILKE, Sir Charles, i, 265, 304
Disgust, by A. C. Swinburne, ii, 94
DOBSON, Mr. Austin, ii, 23
Dodipol, Dr., old English play, ii, 137
Dolores, by A. C. Swinburne, i, 29
DORIAN, Tola, Madame (Princess Mestchersky), letter to, ii, 123, 126

277

INDEX

DOWDEN, Edward, letters to, ii, 166–7, 178–80, 185–6, 227–8
Dramatic Idyls, by Robert Browning, ii, 31
Drayton, ii, 163, 165
Dream of John Ball, A, by William Morris, ii, 258
Dry Sticks, by W. S. Landor, ii, 61
Duchess of Malfi, by Webster, ii, 219–20
Duke of Gandia, The, ii, 118
DUNWICH, ii, 78
Dynasts, The, by T. Hardy, ii, 264–5

Edmund Ironside, old English play, ii, 129
Elegy in a Country Churchyard, by T. Gray, ii, 111
ELLIS, F. S., letters to, i, 89–91
—— references, i, 71, 73, 91–294
EMERSON, R. W., i, 201, 237, 240
Encyclopædia Britannica, Swinburne's articles for, i, 304; ii, 98, 101, 104, 156
Enfants Pauvres, Les, by V. Hugo, Swinburne's translation, i, 69
English Odes, by E. Gosse, ii, 73, 74–5, 83–4
Enoch Arden, by Lord Tennyson, i, 28
Epistle to Lord Stanhope, by W. S. Landor, i, 64, 125
Erechtheus, by A. C. Swinburne, i, 216, 222–3, 236, 248
Essays and Studies, by A. C. Swinburne, i, 176
ETHEREDGE, Sir George, ii, 81, 82–3, 84
Eton, ode by A. C. Swinburne, ii, 213
ETRETAT, i, 292
Eugenia, by G. Chapman, i, 144, 145, 159, 162–3, 165
EURIPIDES, i, 224
Eve of Revolution, The, by A. C. Swinburne, i, 66; ii, 73
Every Man in his Humour, by Ben Jonson, ii, 161–2
Evesham, Vale of, ii, 215

Examiner, The, i, 210, 213, 249, 252, 303

FANTIN LATOUR, M., i, 204, 210
FARRAR, Rev. F. W., ii, 26
Father's Memories of his Child, A, by D. A. Malkin, i, 285
Félise, by A. C. Swinburne, i, 280
FITZGERALD, ii, 244
FLAUBERT, Gustave, i, 240
FLEAY, Rev. F. G., ii, 128
FLORENCE, Swinburne in, i, 17–21
Ford, John, by A. C. Swinburne, i, 295; ii, 110
FORMAN, J. M., "Shelley" by, i, 259
Forsaken Garden, A, by A. C. Swinburne, i, 249
FORSTER, J., i, 41, 115, 116, 123; ii, 75, 86, 90
Fortnightly Review: "Bothwell" reviewed in, Swinburne re reviewers, i, 139–40, 149, 295
—— *Complaint of Mona Lisa* printed in, i, 67; ii, 9
—— *Eve of Revolution* offered to, i, 66
—— *The Last Oracle* offered to, i, 236
—— *North and South* printed in, i, 96, 107
—— Swinburne's description of, i, 214
—— Swinburne's article on *Joseph and his Brethren* in, and correspondence re, i, 173, 197, 205
—— Swinburne's review of *L'Homme qui Rit* for, i, 63, 65, 92
—— Swinburne's review of Nicholas Hannibal in, i, 91
—— Swinburne's review of Rossetti's Poems in, i, 70
—— *The Three Stages of Shakespeare* printed in, i, 195, 227, 302, 308; ii, 31
—— *Vision of Spring in Winter* in, i, 194, 301
—— other contributions to, i, 57; ii, 63, 71, 78, 94, 95, 204, 212
—— references, i, 214, 239

INDEX

Frederick the Great, by Thomas Carlyle, i, 25
FROUDE, Mr. J. A., i, 72; 11, 97
FURNIVAL, F. J., attack on Swinburne, ii, 3, 5, 7, 8-9, 43, 68
—— references, i, 109, 110

Game at Chess, A, by Middleton, ii, 163, 165
GAUTIER, Théophile: Swinburne's Memorial Verses on death of, i, 113, 126-7
——reference in connexion with Poe, i, 131
Gebir, by W. S. Landor, i, 125; ii, 56, 61, 195
GILCHRIST's Life of Blake, i, 284
GLADSTONE, W. E., ii, 26, 55, 227, 228
GLAPTHORNE, i, 154, 155
GLASGOW, ii, 25
Golden House, The, by A. C. Swinburne, MS. of, sent to Hatch, i, 2
GORDON, Sir H., ii, 2
GOSSE, Mr. Edmund, i, 188; ii, 16
—— letters to, i, 58-9, 119-20, 165-6, 171-6, 197-8, 202-3, 209-12, 218-19, 223-7, 233-6, 254-5; ii, 5, 6-7, 8-11, 13, 14-15, 16-18, 20-22, 23-24, 24-25, 27, 37-41, 41-4, 45-6, 46-8, 53-4, 62, 67-70, 73-5, 76, 81-5, 99-100, 105, 110-12, 113, 114, 122-3, 130-1, 132-4, 135-7, 153-5, 155, 172-5, 221-6, 232-3, 235-8, 239-40, 245, 253, 257-8
GRAMMONT, Conte de, ii, 8
GRAY, T., ii, 99, 130
Gray, by E. Gosse, ii, 110, 111
Grenville, Sir Richard, ballad of, by Lord Tennyson, ii, 50
GREVILLE, Mrs., i, 309; ii, 1
GREY, Lord, i, 183
GREY, Lady de, i, 9
GRISWOLD, R. W., slanders Edgar Poe, i, 130, 131, 132, 204
GROSART, Dr. A. B., i, 144, 250, 255, 258; ii, 19, 39, 42, 53, 54, 108, 160, 194

GROSVENOR GALLERY, The, exhibition in, ii, 24

HALLIWELL-PHILLIPS, Mr., i, 308; ii, 107, 204
Halt before Rome, The, by A. C. Swinburne, publication in *Fortnightly Review*, i, 57
Hannibal, by John Nichol, i, 91
Hannibal and Scipio, by Thomas Nabbes (1637), ii, 107
HANSEN, Dr. Adolf, i, 218
HARDY, Mr. Thomas, letters to, ii, 252-3, 264-5
HATCH, Edwin, letters to, i, 6-7
HAWEIS, H. R., letter to, i, 69
HAWTHORNE, Nathaniel, i, 170
Hayley's Ballads, by W. Blake, ii, 25
HAYNE, P. H., letter to, i, 231-3; ii, 139-141
HAZLITT, Carew, ii, 115
HAZLITT, W. C., i, 250
HAZLITT's *Conversations with Northcote*, ii, 238
Hellenics, by W. S. Landor, ii, 58-9
HERBERT OF CHERBURY, Lord, ii, 93, 128
Hero and Leander, by Marlowe, i, 143, 159, 161
Hertha, i, 191
HEYWOOD, i, 153; ii, 149, 159, 161, 223, 225
HOLLINGSHED, revival of *Merry Wives*, Swinburne's song for, i, 303
HOLMES, Augusta, ii, 28, 30
L'Homme qui Rit, by Victor Hugo, i, 63, 65
HORACE, ii, 196-7
HORNE, R. H., i, 133; ii, 140, 147
HOTTEN, J. C., publishing dispute with, i, 45-6, 56-7, 67, 71, 73, 95, 96, 100-6, 290, 292
—— references, ii, 187, 189, 195
HOUGHTON, Lord, letters to, i, 8-10, 17-21, 21-2, 30-1, 47, 54-5, 56-7, 62-3, 250-2, 286, 287-8, 289, 292-3, 296-7, 309; ii, 1-2, 25-6, 30-6, 49-53, 54-6, 58-61, 77-8, 104-5

279

INDEX

HOUGHTON, LORD, references, i, 139, 149; ii, 166, 247
HOWELL, C. A., letters to, i, 28-9, 45-6, 48, 51-2, 55-6, 71, 73-4, 100-2; ii, 21
HUEFFER, F. M., ii, 22
HUGO, Victor, i, 12, 77, 97, 136, 148, 196, 257, 289, 298; ii, 28, 63, 76, 77
Idyllia, by W. S. Landor, ii, 87-8, 195
Imaginary Conversations, by W. S. Landor, ii, 87
Ines de Castro, by W. S. Landor, i, 125
INGRAM, J. H., articles on Poe by, i, 129
—— Poe's works edited by, i, 169, 204
—— letters to, i, 129-34, 136-9, 168-70, 259, 262; ii, 27-8, 28-9, 265-8
IONIDES, Mrs., letter to, ii, 125-6
Iphigenia in Tauris, Goethe's, i, 25
Ippolito di Este, by W. S. Landor, i, 125
IRVING, Sir Henry, i, 309; ii, 152
ISLE, Rouget de l', i, 211

Jack Straw's Life and Death (1593), by John Dancer, ii, 109
Jacobean Poets, The, by Edmund Gosse, ii, 235
Jacques le Fataliste, by Diderot, i, 306
JEFFERIES, Richard, ii, 139
JOHN WOODVIL, ii, 121
JONSON, Ben, i, 158; ii, 161, 192
Joseph and His Brethren, by C. J. Wells, i, 8, 192, 197, 205, 238; ii, 17
JOWETT, Benjamin, i, 84, 87, 89, 90, 127, 135, 268-70; ii, 1, 88, 195

KEATS, Swinburne's article on, ii, 82
—— memorial to, ii, 239-40
KELMSCOTT PRESS, ii, 234, 243, 250, 251

KENEALY, Dr., i, 177
KING, Mr., i, 94, 96, 197-8
King Erik, by Edmund Gosse, i, 210, 233-4
King or no King, A, ii, 121
KINGSLEY, H., ii, 233
KIRKUP, S., letters to, i, 281-2, 283-5, 290-1
—— portrait of Lady J. Swinburne by, i, 283
KNIGHT, Joseph, letters to, i, 79-82, 222-3, 303-4
—— references, i, 77, 95, 96
KNOWLES, Sir James, ii, 231

Lady of Pleasure, The, by Shirley, ii, 152
LA FONTAINE, *Contes* de, ii, 26
LAMB, Charles, centenary of, proposed celebration, i, 171-2, 177
—— Moxon's edition of works of, ii, 121
—— poetry of, Swinburne's admiration for, i, 53
—— sonnet to Barry Cornwall, Swinburne's verses after reading, i, 60
—— references, i, 117; ii, 23, 102, 107, 110, 115, 121, 144, 148
LANDOR, R. E., ii, 91
LANDOR, Walter Savage, appearance of, i, 193
—— centenary of, proposed celebration, i, 171-2
—— circumstances leading to departure of, from England, Swinburne's account, i, 121-3; ii, 91-2
—— death of, Swinburne's sorrow, i, 24
—— first collected edition of works of, date, i, 126-7
—— first publications of, ii, 86-87, 195
—— Forster's biography of, ii, 86
—— Lord Houghton introduces Swinburne to, ii, 77
—— Lord Houghton's selections from, ii, 47, 58-60

INDEX

LANDOR, Walter Savage, Mrs. Lynn Linton's articles on, ii, 86, 92
—— *Moral Epistle to Earl Stanhope* (1795), by, i, 64, 125
—— pamphlet by, i, 21
—— poems of, Swinburne's appreciation, i, 19, 172
—— prose palinode on Byron, ii, 87–88
—— *Simonidea*, discovery of copy, ii, 228, 239
—— E. C. Stedman's article on, and selections from poems of, i, 115–9, 121–7
—— Swinburne's Latin elegiacs on, i, 127
—— Swinburne's Memorial Poem on, ii, 59, 70, 78
—— unpublished MSS. of, i, 124, 254
—— visit to, i, 17–20
—— references, i, 13, 15–18, 151, 193; ii, 84, 194–5, 238
Laon and Cythna, by P. B. Shelley, i, 302; ii, 167
Last Fruit, by W. S. Landor, ii, 61, 90
Last Oracle, The, by A. C. Swinburne, i, 236–7, 253, 304–5
Latin Idyls, by W. S. Landor, ii, 195
Laugh and Lie Down; or, The World's Folly, i, 110
Lays and Legends, by E. Nesbit, ii, 177
LEADER, TEMPLE, i, 20
LEE, Sir Sidney, letters to, ii, 200–1, 204–6, 252, 257
LEMERRE, M., i, 99
Lesbia Brander, by A. C. Swinburne, i, 50
LESCUREL, Jehannot de, ii, 11
Letters to the Press, by A. C. Swinburne, ii, 3, 12
Letting of Humour's Blood in the Head Vein, The, by Samuel Rowlands, ii, 53
LEWES, G. H., i, 24, 288; ii, 248, 263
Liberty, by J. S. Mill, i, 136

LINTON, Mrs. Lynn, ii, 86
LISLE, Leconte de, i, 240
Literature and Dogma, by Matthew Arnold, Swinburne's admiration for, i, 108, 190
LOCKER, Frederick, letters to, i, 83–5, 88–9; ii, 6
—— reference, i, 131
LOCKER, Lady Charlotte, i, 84
Locrine, ii, 253–4
LODGE, Thomas, ii, 122
London Magazine, ii, 113
LONGFELLOW, i, 181, 192
Lost Tales of Miletus, by Sir E. B. Lytton, i, 35
Love Laid his Sleepless Head, by A. C. Swinburne, i, 303
Love's Cross Currents, by A. C. Swinburne. See *A Year's Letters by Mrs. Horace Manners*.
Love's Cure; or, The Martial Maid, by Fletcher, ii, 180
Love's Horoscope, by T. Crashaw, ii, 132
LOVELACE, Lord, ii, 270
Low, Sampson, letter to, i, 61–2
LOWELL, J. R., i, 216; ii, 102
Lust's Dominion, ii, 148, 152
Lycidas, by John Milton, ii, 48
Lyrical Ballads, by W. Wordsworth, ii, 194
Lyrics from the Dramatists, by A. H. Bullen, ii, 208
Lyrics from Elizabethan Songbooks, by A. H. Bullen, ii, 180–1, 184–6, 203
LYTTON, Lord, advice *re Poems and Ballads*, i, 40, 45
—— letters to, i, 35–6, 40–5
—— reference, ii, 168

MACCOLL, Norman, ii, 8
—— letters to, ii, 2–4, 12]
MACKENZIE, letter to, i, 150–1
MADDEN, Right Hon. H. D., letter to, ii, 262–3
MAGGI, Prof., i, 210
Maid's Metamorphosis, The, in Collection of Old English Plays, by A. H. Bullen, ii, 108

INDEX

MALLARMÉ, Stéphane, letters to, i, 226-7, 252-4, 265-70, 274-6, 281-2
—— references, i, 154, 225, 234, 287
MANET, M., i, 210, 220, 226, 227, 244
MARLOWE, Christopher, i, 179-80, 190; ii, 147, 150, 200, 205-6, 267-8
MARSTON, Dr., i, 133
MARSTON, John, ii, 17, 149, 159, 160, 181, 187, 204
MARSTON, Philip Bourke, letters to, ii, 177-8
—— references, i, 83, 187; ii, 136, 182
Martial Maid, The, by Fletcher, ii, 180
MARTINEAU, Dr., ii, 256
Mary Stuart: a Tragedy, by A. C. Swinburne, ii, 31, 49, 96, 101, 102, 185
MARZIALS, T., i, 167, 256
MASON, E., ii, 141
Masque of Anarchy, The, by P. B. Shelley, ii, 191, 195, 229
MASSEY, Gerald, letter to, i, 52-3
MASSINGER, ii, 113, 121, 127, 131, 138, 153
MAZZINI, G., *Songs before Sunrise*, dedicated to, i, 75
—— Swinburne consults with, *re* invitation to enter Parliament, i, 188
—— Swinburne's meeting with, i, 267, 274; ii, 78
MENDES, Catulle, i, 229, 240, 246, 247
MENKEN, Adah Isaacs, i, 60
MENTONE, i, 10-11
MEREDITH, George, i, 9, 35, 38, 239; ii, 187
MÉRIMÉE, Prosper, ii, 22
Merope, Arnold's, i, 25
MICHAELIS, Th., visit to Swinburne as representative of Victor Hugo, i, 140; reference, i, 299
Microcosmus, by Thomas Nabbes, ii, 184

MIDDLETON, ii, 120, 129, 144, 149, 156, 159, 163, 221
Midsummer Holiday and Other Poems, by A. C. Swinburne, ii, 141
MILL, John Stuart, autobiography of, i, 136
MILNES, R. M. (*see* Lord Houghton)
MINTO, W., i, 166, 177
MIRABEAU, Sir J. Swinburne's friendship with, i, 183-4
Miscellanies, by A. C. Swinburne, ii, 71, 95.
Misérables, Les, by Victor Hugo, ii, 77
MOHL, Madame von, i, 54
MONTAUVERT, Chartreuse Convent at, ii, 167, 179
MONTÉGUT, article on Kingsley, Swinburne's praise of, i, 6
MORLEY, Lord, letters to, i, 63-66, 70, 91-3, 107-09, 112-14, 134, 136, 139-40, 148-9, 236-40, 294-6, 298, 302, 304-8; ii, 63-7, 71-2, 80-1, 94-7, 142
—— editorship of *Fortnightly Review*, i, 214-15
MORRIS, William, i, 2-7, 132; ii, 143, 145, 151, 258, 270
—— letters to, ii, 234, 243
MOXON & CO., Messrs., i, 39, 42-3, 49, 125
Muleasses, by Mason, ii, 172

NABBES, T., ii, 107, 109, 183, 257
NASH, ii, 221, 224
Neveu de Rameau, i, 240, 306
NEWMAN, Cardinal, extract from letter from, Swinburne's criticism, i, 234-6
—— Swinburne's sonnet on, i, 226-7
New Trick to Cheat the Devil, A, by R. Davenport, i, 255; ii, 145, 211
NICHOL, John, i, 3, 265, 272; ii, 25, 80
Nineteenth Century, The, ii, 117, 187, 204, 231
Nobody and Somebody (1600), ii, 23

INDEX

Nocturne, by A. C. Swinburne: publication of, in *La République des Lettres*, i, 228–32, 239, 243–5, 251, 307
North and South, by A. C. Swinburne, i, 96, 107
North Sea, By the, by A. C. Swinburne, ii, 70
NORTHCOTE'S *Fables*, ii, 237
Note on Character of Mary Q. of Scots, by A. C. Swinburne, ii, 95, 96
Notes and Queries, ii, 121

Ode on Proclamation of French Republic, by A. C. Swinburne, i, 71, 72
Ode on the Insurrection in Candia, by A. C. Swinburne, ii, 73
Ode to Brutus, by Cowley, ii, 84
Ode to Joseph Ablett, by W. S. Landor, ii, 74
Ode to Miletus, by W. S. Landor, ii, 74
Ode to Spring, by Warton, ii, 84
Omar Khayyám, by E. FitzGerald, ii, 243–4
Ompetrailles le Tombeau des Lutteurs, by Léon Cladel, ii, 51
Once a Week, Swinburne's sestina in, ii, 6–7, 10
On the Cliffs, by A. C. Swinburne, ii, 48
ORLOFF, Princess, i, 92
O'SHAUGHNESSY, Arthur, i, 167
Outlanders, The, ii, 145

Pall Mall Gazette, The, i, 258, 262; ii, 168
PARIS, Swinburne's impressions of, i, 13
Parliament of Fowls, The, by G. Chaucer, ii, 240
PATER, Walter, i, 107–8
PAYNE, J. B., letters to, i, 22–3, 39–40
—— references, i, 43–6, 253
PERIE, R., letter to, i, 212–15
Philip van Artevelde, by Sir Henry Taylor, i, 135; ii, 96, 101

Phocœans, by W. S. Landor, i, 125
Phœnix and Turtle, by W. Shakespeare, ii, 43
Pierce Pennilesse, by Nash, ii, 221
Pietro of Abano, by R. Browning, ii, 198
Pilgrims, by A. C. Swinburne, ii, 28
POE, Edgar A., i, 129–34, 136–7, 169–70, 204, 207, 220, 259, 262; ii, 140
POEL, W., letter to, ii, 219–20
Poems, by D. G. Rossetti (1870), Swinburne's review of, in *Fortnightly Review*, i, 70
Poems and Ballads, by A. C. Swinburne, i, 40–3, 56; ii, 2, 25, 33, 69, 255–6
POLIDORI, T. W., ii, 233
Poor Man's Comfort, The, by Robert Daborne, ii, 107
POWELL, G., i, 82
PRIMROSE LEAGUE, ii, 146
PROCTER, Bryan Waller, letter to, i, 60–1
PROCTOR, Mrs., ii, 1, 55
Prometheus, Shelley's, i, 24
Proverbs in Porcelain, by Mr. Austin Dobson, ii, 13
PURNELL, Thomas, letters to, i, 30, 60, 67–8, 72, 74–6, 86, 87–8, 93–7, 177–8, 260–2, 263–76
—— reference, ii, 117

Quarterly Review, The, ii, 77, 172, 173–4
Quatre Vents de l'Esprit, Les, by V. Hugo, i, 149, 300
Quatrevingt-Treize, by Victor Hugo, i, 148
Queen Mary, by A. Tennyson, i, 216
Queen Mother and Rosamund, The, by A. C. Swinburne, i, 11, 23, 24, 46

Raven, The, by E. A. Poe, i, 259
READE, Charles, ii, 32

INDEX

Recollections of the Last Days of Shelley and Byron, by Trelawny, i, 217
REFORM LEAGUE, invitation from, to Swinburne to sit in Parliament, i, 187
Regret, by A. C. Swinburne, publication in *Fortnightly Review*, i, 57
Religions et Religion, by V. Hugo, ii, 63, 65
Reminiscences, by Thomas Carlyle, ii, 103
Report of the First Anniversary Meeting of the Newest Shakespeare Society, by A. C. Swinburne, i, 249, 252
République des Lettres, La, i, 137, 228–32, 239, 243–5, 251
Revenger's Tragedy, The, by Cyril Tourneur, i, 109, 111, 250, 257; ii, 17, 115, 224
Review of Hogg's Memoirs of Prince Alexy Haimatoff, edited by Mr. T. J. Wise, ii, 166
Revolt of Islam, The, by P. B. Shelley, ii, 167
RICE, Sarah Sigourney, letter to, i, 220–1
—— reference, i, 137
Ring and the Book, The, by R. B. Browning, i, 62
RITCHIE, Lady, letter to, ii, 272
Rizpah, by Lord Tennyson, ii, 78
Roi s'amuse, Le, by Victor Hugo, ii, 123
Roman de la Rose, i, 284
ROSSETTI, Christina, i, 76; ii, 232
ROSSETTI, D. G., drawing of Swinburne for frontispiece to Italian translations, i, 9
—— references, i, 8, 9, 11, 14, 46, 70, 108, 202, 229, 242, 282; ii, 7, 10, 58, 60, 191, 232, 244
ROSSETTI, William Michael, letter to, i, 76–8
—— references, i, 14, 38, 51, 100, 131, 165–6, 211, 217, 241; ii, 22
ROWLANDS, Samuel, in Gosse's edition of, ii, 53

RUSKIN, John, letter to, i, 14–16
—— references, i, 38, 47, 48; ii, 256

DE SADE, Marquis, i, 9, 293; ii, 32, 50
Sailing of the Swallow, The, by A. C. Swinburne, ii, 4
SALA, i, 71
SANDYS, F., ii, 187–8
Satire on Ben Jonson, A, by G. Chapman, i, 144
Saturday Review, i, 4, 308; ii, 77, 97
Satyr on Satirists, by W. S. Landor, ii, 60
Savonarola, by W. S. Landor, Swinburne's possession of copies of, i, 124
SCOTT, Sir W., ii, 53
SCOTT, William Bell, i, 167, 171; ii, 226
Scribner's Magazine, i, 128
Second Maiden's Tragedy, by G. Chapman, i, 144, 153, 157, 160, 174; ii, 129
Sestina, by A. C. Swinburne, ii, 6–7, 10
Seventeenth Century Studies, by Edmund Gosse, ii, 135
Shadow of Night, The, by G. Chapman, i, 153
SHAKESPEARE, William, i, 174–5
Shakespeare, Three Stages of, by A. C. Swinburne, i, 175, 227, 300, 302, 308, 31, 39
SHARP, William, letter to, ii, 259–60
SHELLEY, i, 4, 172, 202–3, 217; ii, 166, 167, 171, 179
Shepherd's Holiday, The, by Walter Montague, ii, 197
SHEPHERD, R. H., editions of Decker and Heywood by, i, 153
—— letters to, i, 142–5, 145–8, 151–65; ii, 79, 170
—— Swinburne's advice to, re complete edition of Chapman's works, i, 143–4, 145–8, 151–65
—— reference, i, 191
Shirley, ii, 149, 152, 159

284

INDEX

Short Notes on English Poets, by A. C. Swinburne, ii, 71
SHORTER, Mr. Clement K., letters to, ii, 233, 243, 246-9, 256, 261-2
Siena, by A. C. Swinburne, i, 292
Sieste de Jeanne, La, by Victor Hugo, Swinburne's essay on, ii, 3
Simonidea, by W. S. Landor, ii, 90, 228
Sir Hugh the Heron, by D. G. Rossetti, ii, 192
Sir John van Olden Barnavelt, edited by A. H. Bullen, ii, 128, 131, 132, 138
Sisters, The, by A. C. Swinburne, ii, 218
SMITH, Elder & Co., Messrs., letter to, ii, 209-10
SOLOMON, S., ii, 46
Song for the Centenary of Landor, The, by A. C. Swinburne, ii, 70
Song in Season, A, by A. C. Swinburne, ii, 132
Song of Italy, by A. C. Swinburne, arrangements for American publication of, i, 74-5
Songs before Sunrise, i, 74, 208
Songs of Two Nations, by A. C. Swinburne, i, 176-7
Songs of Innocence, by W. Blake, ii, 186
Songs of the Springtides, by A. C. Swinburne, ii, 50, 55, 94
Sonnets on English Dramatic Poets, by A. C. Swinburne, ii, 105
Sophonisba, by John Marston, ii, 181
Sordello, by R. Browning, i, 3-4, 7
Spectator, The, i, 226; ii, 94
SPEDDING, Mr., i, 302
Stances à Collette, by A. C. Swinburne, ii, 35-6
STANHOPE, Lady H., ii, 264
St. Anthony, by G. Flaubert, i, 149
STEDMAN, Edmund C., article by, i, 208
—— Landor selections edited by, i, 115-9
—— letters to, i, 15-9, 120-8, 179-94, 215-8; ii, 100-4

STEDMAN, Edmund C., references, ii, 35, 133
Studies in Prose and Poetry, by A. C. Swinburne, ii, 241
Studies in Song, by A. C. Swinburne, ii, 70, 74
SULLIVAN, Sir Arthur, ii, 231
SWINBURNE, Admiral, death of, ii, 1-2; parentage, i, 182
SWINBURNE, Algernon Charles, announces progress of *Rosamond*, i, 1-2
—— admiration of Morris's *Defence of Guenevere*, i, 1-2
—— *The Golden House*, i, 2
—— at work on *Tristram*, i, 4
—— ironic description of his own work, i, 4
—— plans *The Albigenses*, i, 5
—— articles on Wells's *Joseph and his Brethren*, i, 8
—— Rossetti's drawing of, for frontispiece to Italian translations, i, 9
—— work on *Chastelard*, i, 9
—— early poems and stories, i, 11
—— discusses profession, i, 12
—— in Florence, visits W. S. Landor, i, 17-21
—— on William Blake, i, 281-2, 284
—— on Transmigration of Souls, i, 284
—— describes writing of *Atalanta in Calydon*, i, 23-4
—— delight in Carlyle's *Frederick the Great*, i, 25-6
—— admiration for Madox Brown's pictures, i, 27
—— criticism of Tennyson's *Selections*, i, 27
—— additions to *Dolores*, i, 29
—— *Atalanta* and *Chastelard*, reception of, i, 30, 33, 286
—— reply to charges of intemperance, i, 286-8
—— publication of *Poems and Ballads*, 1866, unfavourable reception and correspondence *re* publishers' action, i, 40, 41-2, 49

INDEX

SWINBURNE, Algernon Charles, book on Blake, i, 51, 290
— interest in Massey's study of Shakespeare's sonnets and Lamb's poetry, i, 52-3
— ill health, i, 54-5
— accident to, i, 60
— Étretât swimming adventure, i, 292
— undertakes to edit Coleridge's poems, i, 61
— delight in *The Ring and the Book*, i, 62
— Reviews Victor Hugo's *L'Homme qui Rit*, i, 63
— offers *The Eve of Revolution* to *Fortnightly Review*, i, 66
— dispute with Hotten *re* publishing agreement, i, 67, 71, 73
— translates Victor Hugo's *Les Enfants Pauvres* for *Cassell's Magazine*, i, 69
— reviews Rossetti's poems in *Fortnightly Review*, i, 70
— writes *Ode on Proclamation of French Republic*, i, 71, 72
— publication of *Songs before Sunrise* and arrangement for American issue, i, 74, 294
— proposes public demonstration on occasion of Victor Hugo's visit to London, i, 77-82
— at work on *Bothwell*, i, 83
— *Tristram and Iseult: Prelude of an Unfinished Poem*, printed, and correspondence *re* its publication, i, 85, 86, 88, 94
— pamphlet *Under the Microscope*, i, 89
— reviews Nichol's *Hannibal* in *Fortnightly Review*, i, 91
— poem on Gautier, i, 92-3
— *Before Sunset*, printed in *Athenæum*, i, 93
— dispute with Hotten *re* transference of books to Chapman & Hall, i, 95-6, 100-1
— *North and South* printed in *Fortnightly Review*, i, 96, 107

SWINBURNE, Algernon Charles, dedicatory sonnet to *Bothwell*, i, 97-9
— progress with *Bothwell*, i, 97, 106, 113-14
— admiration for Pater's work; reference to Pater's avowal of Swinburne's influence on him, i, 107-8
— advice *re* Churton Collins's proposal to edit plays of Cyril Tourneur, i, 109-11
— negotiations for future publication with Chapman & Hall, i, 112-13
— on Stedman's selections from Landor's poems, i, 115-19
— contributions to *Le Tombeau de Théophile Gautier*, i, 118, 126
— appreciation of Stedman's article on Landor in *Victorian Poets*, i, 121-6
— on W. S. Landor and circumstances leading to his departure from England, i, 121-2
— on Browning's possession of some unpublished MSS. of Landor, i, 124; ii, 39
— on first editions of Landor's poems, i, 125-6
— views on modern classic verses, i, 126
— elegy on Baudelaire, i, 128
— help in formation of Poe Committee, and congratulations *re* Mr. Ingram's refutation of slanders on Poe, i, 129-34, 136-7
— announces conclusion of *Bothwell*, i, 134-5, 295
— consents to election to committee for Byron monument, i, 138
— *re* the reviewing of *Bothwell* by Lord Houghton, i, 139, 148-9, 296-7
— assistance to R. H. Shepherd's edition of Chapman, i, 143-4, 151-2, 152-65
— on Poet Laureateship, i, 150
— book on Chapman, i, 163-4, 173-4, 191-2, 299

286

INDEX

SWINBURNE, Algernon Charles, on Ingram's edition of Poe's works, i, 168–70
—— contrasts Poe with Hawthorne, i, 170
—— proposes celebration of Lamb and Landor centenary, i, 171–2, 177
—— objects to classification of Landor with Catullus, i, 172–3
—— on Landor's verse and prose, i, 173
—— article on *Joseph and his Brethren*, i, 173, 195, 197, 205–6
—— essay on metrical progress of Shakespeare, i, 175, 191, 194, 227, 300, 302; ii, 30, 39, 50
—— discusses title for *Songs of Two Nations*, i, 175, 176
—— *Essays and Studies* going through press, i, 176
—— on American poetry, i, 180–1, 215–16
—— visits abroad, i, 192
—— payments for his books, in England and America, i, 192–3
—— gives account of family history, i, 182–5
—— fondness for children and very old people, i, 193
—— personal history, i, 185–8
—— religious opinions, i, 188–90
—— on his early poems, i, 191
—— opinions of Rossetti's translations, i, 202–3
—— on America's projected monument to Poe, i, 207, 220–1, 262
—— disappointment concerning lack of sympathy in America for his republican ideals, i, 208
—— opinion as to English reviews and periodicals, i, 213–15
—— at work on *Erechtheus*, i, 216–17, 222
—— essay on Shelley, i, 217
—— on *Athenæum's* and *Spectator's* reviews of *Erechtheus*, i, 224–7
—— sonnets on Newman and Carlyle, i, 226–7

SWINBURNE, Algernon Charles, appreciation of Gosse's *King Erik*, i, 233–4
—— on religion and eroticism, i, 235
—— offers *The Last Oracle* to *Fortnightly Review*, i, 236–8, 304–5
—— contributions to *La République des Lettres*, i, 239–40, 243–5, 251
—— translations of Villon, i, 241–2
—— essay on Blake for *République des Lettres*, i, 245–6
—— *A Forsaken Garden*, i, 249
—— *Report of First Anniversary Meeting of the Newest Shakespeare Society*, i, 249, 252
—— connexion with Byron Committee, i, 250–1
—— illness of, from perfume of Indian lilies, i, 254–5
—— articles on Congreve, i, 256
—— *Ballad of Bulgarie*, its chance of getting printed, i, 258, 262, 265
—— *A Year's Letters*, by Mrs. Horace Manners, i, 260–2, 263–76
—— reference to his meeting with Mazzini, i, 267–74
—— *re* his father's death, ii, 1–2
—— essay on *La Sieste de Jeanne*, by Victor Hugo, in *Athenæum*, ii, 3
—— Furnivall quarrel, ii, 3, 4, 7, 8–9, 43
—— *The Sailing of the Swallow*, printed in the *Gentleman's Magazine*, ii, 4
—— his invention of rhyming sestina, ii, 6–7, 9
—— article on Zola's *L'Assommoir*, ii, 12
—— essay on Charlotte Brontë, ii, 13, 172
—— project for *Dictionary of the English Drama*, ii, 14, 15, 22, 47
—— on Cyril Tourneur's plays, ii, 17, 18–19
—— *Poems and Ballads, Second Series*, completed for press, ii, 25

INDEX

SWINBURNE, Algernon Charles, Mlle. Holmès's translation of his works, reference to, ii, 27-8, 30
—— Victor Hugo's invitation to Paris, Swinburne's delight at, ii, 29-30
—— *re* project of selections from *The English Poets*, ii, 37, 41-2
—— *re* scandalous charges, ii, 45-6
—— *re* wish to undertake selections from Landor, ii, 47-8
—— writes *On the Cliffs*, ii, 49
—— on Tennyson's ballad on Sir Richard Grenville, ii, 50
—— on publication of *Songs of the Springtides*, ii, 50-5
—— announces new domestic arrangements, ii, 52-3
—— on Gosse's edition of works of Samuel Rowlands, ii, 53-4
—— on *Alcilia*, reprinted by Dr. A. Grosart, ii, 54
—— on Lord Houghton's selections from Landor, ii, 58, 59, 60
—— reviews Victor Hugo's *Religions et Religion*, ii, 63, 65
—— on quarrel with Furnivall, ii, 67-8
—— *Studies in Song* and *Song for Centenary of Landor*, ii, 70
—— *Short Notes on English Poets*, ii, 71-2
—— choice of odes for *English Odes*, ii, 73-7, 83-5
—— Memorial Poem on Landor, ii, 77-8
—— on Sir G. Etheredge and Restoration Dramatists, ii, 81, 82
—— articles on Landor by himself and others, ii, 86
—— admiration of Landor's prose palinode on Byron's death, ii, 87, 88
—— on *Note on the Character of Mary Queen of Scots*, ii, 96, 97, 98
—— Sir H. Taylor's praise of Mary Stuart, Swinburne's satisfaction, ii, 96, 101

SWINBURNE, Algernon Charles, *Tristram of Lyonesse and Other Poems*, ii, 98, 102, 105
—— at work on *Life of Mary Queen of Scots*, ii, 97-8, 101-2, 104-5, 156
—— on A. H. Bullen's *Collection of Old English Plays*, ii, 106-9, 119-20, 127-30, 137-8
—— criticism of *English Men of Letters*, edited by John Morley, ii, 110
—— on authenticity of autographic corrections in volume of Massinger's poems, ii, 113
—— his wish to write the life and death of Cæsar Borgia, ii, 118
—— *Notes and Queries*, concerning Lamb, ii, 120-22
—— in Paris for 50th anniversary of *Le Roi s'amuse*, ii, 122-3
—— his acknowledgment of French translation of *The Statue of Victor Hugo*, ii, 123
—— on Shakespeare's use of prose and verse, ii, 124
—— at work on *A Century of Roundels*, ii, 132
—— on E. C. Stedman's indigent circumstances, ii, 133
—— on Byron's and Poe's poetry, ii, 140-1
—— on Christmas Carols, ii, 143
—— recommends further publications of Restoration Plays, ii, 145, 151-3, 160, 196-7, 208, 209
—— *re* utilization of his verses by Primrose League, ii, 146
—— *re* works of Christopher Marlowe, ii, 147
—— criticism of Walt Whitman, ii, 154
—— on receipt of Stevenson's *A Child's Garden of Verses*, ii, 155
—— acknowledges receipt of Bullen's *Middleton*, ii, 156
—— on reprint of Shelley's *Review of Hogg's Memoirs*, ii, 166
—— on Shelley's signature in visitors' book at Chartreuse Convent, ii, 167, 179

INDEX

SWINBURNE, Algernon Charles, admiration for Prof. Collins' Papers on Education, ii, 168–9
—— on attack upon him and Mr. Gosse in *Quarterly Review*, ii, 172
—— on *Lays and Legends*, by E. Nesbit, ii, 177
—— his pleasure at receipt of E. Dowden's *Life of Shelley*, ii, 179
—— thanks for Bullen's Lyrics from Elizabethan Songbooks, ii, 180–1, 186–7, 204
—— acknowledges receipt of Bullen's edition of Marston, ii, 181
—— on Bullen's *Works of Thomas Nabbes*, ii, 183
—— on his correspondence with Sir Henry Taylor, ii, 185–6
—— on his stanzas on F. Sandy's drawing of "Cleopatra," ii, 187
—— on his early works, ii, 190–1, 239
—— on his collection of rare volumes, ii, 193
—— on William Bullen's *Dialogue*, ii, 197–9, 201–2
—— on his appointment on Committee for memorial to Christopher Marlowe, ii, 200
—— on the Irish question, ii, 202
—— approves of choice of Canterbury for memorial to Marlowe, ii, 205–7
—— declines invitation to attend R. Browning's funeral, ii, 209, 217
—— thanks to A. H. Bullen for his edition of Davenport's works, ii, 211
—— walking in Wye Valley, ii, 214–15
—— on his unpublished poem on Grace Darling, and *The Sisters*, ii, 217–18
—— pleasure at Poel's production of *Duchess of Malfi*, ii, 219
—— on Nash's works, ii, 221–2, 223, 224
—— at work on study of Heywood's works, ii, 224, 225–6

SWINBURNE, Algernon Charles, on his early friendship with Sir George Young, ii, 224, 225
—— on Cyril Tourneur's merits as dramatist, ii, 226
—— writes *The Union*, "a Song for Irish Unionists," ii, 227–8, 230–2
—— on discovery of copy of *Simonidea*, by W. S. Landor, ii, 228, 239
—— on *Hazlitt's Conversations with Northcote*, ii, 238
—— on American tribute to Keats, ii, 240
—— correcting proofs of *Studies in Prose and Poetry*, ii, 241–2
—— on Omar Khayyám, ii, 243–4
—— his pleasure at J. T. Wise's gift of Brontë manuscripts, ii, 249
—— his pleasure at S. C. Cockerell's gift, *Laudis beatae Mariae virginis*, and leaves of Kelmscott *Froissart*, ii, 250–1
—— on Thomas Hardy's *Wessex Poems*, ii, 252–3
—— discussion of *Locrine*, ii, 253–4
—— on merits of *The Armada* versus *Atalanta* for use in schools, ii, 255–6
—— in praise of Sir Richard Burton, ii, 257–8
—— reads William Morris's *Life of John Bull*, ii, 258
—— criticism of W. Sharp's *Selections from Swinburne's Poems*, ii, 259–60
—— on Dora Sigerson's Poems, ii, 261
—— on receipt of *The Diary of Master William Silence*, ii, 262
—— on Tolstoy's admiration of Charles Dickens, ii, 263
—— on Thomas Hardy's *The Dynasts*, ii, 264
—— praise of J. H. Ingram's *Christopher Marlowe and his Associates*, ii, 266-8
—— sends manuscript of *Astrophel* to S. C. Cockerell, ii, 269

INDEX

SWINBURNE, Algernon Charles, on receipt of supposed portrait of Cæsar Borgia, ii, 269
—— on receipt of Lord Lovelace's *Astarte*, ii, 270
—— refuses offer of honorary degree at Oxford, ii, 271
—— on Miss Coleridge's poems, ii, 272-3
SWINBURNE, Lady J., ancestry of, i, 184-5
—— portrait of, i, 283
SWINBURNE, Julia, i, 25, 34
SWINBURNE, Sir J. (grandfather of A. C. S.), birth and history of, i, 182-4
SWINBURNE, Mrs., companion of Gray, ii, 99
Swinburniana, by R. H. Shepherd, ii, 191

Tamburlaine the Great, the First Part of, by Marlowe, i, 155; ii, 266
TAUCHNITZ selections from Swinburne, ii, 259
TAYLOR, Bayard, i, 61, 74
—— Sir Henry, ii, 96, 101, 185
Tempest, The, ii, 109
TENNYSON, Lord, i, 5, 19, 27, 34, 68, 137, 288; ii, 33, 50, 55, 78, 117
THACKERAY, Bibliography of, ii, 79
Thalassius, by A. C. Swinburne, ii, 70
Thanatopsis, by Bryant, i, 180
Theresa, St., i, 235
THOMAS, F. D., letter to, ii, 146
Times, The, ii, 33-4, 77
'Tis Merry when Gossips Meet, by Samuel Rowlands, ii, 53
Titus Andronicus, ii, 150
TOLSTOY, ii, 264
Tombeau de Théophile Gautier, Le, Swinburne's contributions to, i, 118-19
Tottenham Court, play by Thomas Nabbes, ii, 109, 183-4
TOURNEUR, Cyril, i, 109-11, 249-50, 257-8; ii, 17, 124, 225, 226

Traitor, The, by Shirley, ii, 152
Transformed Metamorphosis, by C. Tourneur, i, 110; ii, 17, 18
TRELAWNY, i, 138, 193, 217, 251
TREVELYAN, Paulina, Lady, letters to, i, 10-14, 14-15, 15-16, 23-8, 31-5, 37-8
—— Sir Walter, ii, 1
Tristram and Iseult: Prelude of an Unfinished Poem, by A. C. Swinburne, i, 85, 86, 299
Tristram and Iseult, by A. C. Swinburne, i, 299
Tristram of Lyonesse and other Poems, by A. C. Swinburne, ii, 98, 102, 105, 116
Tristram Shandy, ii, 215
Twilight of the Lords, The, by A. C. Swinburne, ii, 146
Two Wise Men and all the rest Fools, by G. Chapman, i, 144, 154, 156

Under the Microscope, by A. C. Swinburne, i, 89, 94, 111
Unfortunate Mother, The, by Thomas Nabbes, ii, 184
Union, The, by A. C. Swinburne, ii, 227-8, 231-2
Unknown Eros, The, by Coventry Patmore, ii, 113

VACQUERIE, Auguste, letter to, ii, 57
—— reference, i, 251, 253, 282
VERONESE, Paolo, *Martyrdom of St. Justine*, by, Swinburne's comment on, i, 21
Victor Hugo in Exile, To, by A. C. Swinburne, ii, 75, 76
VILLON, Swinburne's and Rossetti's translations of, i, 241-2
Vision of Spring in Winter, by A. C. Swinburne, i, 194, 301

WARD, Mr. T. Humphry, ii, 47
WARD, Prof. Sir Adolphus W., ii, 47-48
Wars of Cyrus, anonymous play (1594), ii, 106, 119, 145

INDEX

WATTS, Walter Theodore (afterwards Watts-Dunton), letters to, ii, 214-16, 240-2
—— management of Swinburne's literary affairs, i, 95-6, 100-6
—— references, i, 95-6, 100, 171, 199, 249, 268; ii, 19, 22, 23, 41, 45, 48, 55, 62, 67, 82, 85, 93, 104, 114, 133, 157, 168, 174, 177, 190, 191, 208, 222, 229, 239, 247, 257, 262, 273
Well at the World's End, The, by W. Morris, ii, 258
WELLS, C. J., letter from, i, 201
—— letter to, i, 200
—— references, i, 173, 195, 197, 199, 205-6, 238
Wessex Poems, by Thomas Hardy, ii, 252-3
WHISTLER, J. M., i, 204, 210
WHITE, David, i, 91
White Czar and Rizpah, The, by A. C. Swinburne, ii, 26
WHITMAN, Walt, i, 47, 181, 213, 251; ii, 104, 153
WHITTIER, J. G., i, 216
WILDE, Oscar, ii, 103

WILKES, i, 184
WILKINSON, J. J. G., i, 291
WILLIAMS, W. S., letters to, i, 199, 205-6, 229-31
Willobie His Avisa, published by A. B. Grosart, ii, 39-40
WILSON, John, ii, 82
WISE, Mr. Thomas James, letters to, ii, 166, 169, 171, 187-96, 228-29, 238-9, 249-50
WOLFE, J., and Gray's *Elegy*, ii, 111
Woman who went to Hell, The, by Dora Sigerson, ii, 261
Word for the Country, A, by A. C. Swinburne, ii, 146
WORDSWORTH, Swinburne and, ii, 111
World, The, ii, 20

YARINGTON, R., ii, 164
YATES, ii, 20
Year's Letters, A, by Mrs. Horace Manners, by A. C. Swinburne, letters *re* terms for publication of, i, 260-2, 263-276, 291-304
YOUNG, Sir George, ii, 224-225

711
9146 5